FREEDOM COMES TO MISSISSIPPI
The story of Reconstruction

FREEDOM COMES TO MISSISSIPPI
The story of Reconstruction

BY MILTON MELTZER

illustrated with prints and photographs

 **Follett Publishing Company**

Chicago

Books by Milton Meltzer

History

A Pictorial History of the Negro in America (with Langston Hughes)
In Their Own Words: A History of the American Negro, 3 volumes.
Black Magic: A Pictorial History of the Negro in American
      Entertainment (with Langston Hughes)
Time of Trial, Time of Hope: The Negro in America, 1919-1941 (with
      August Meier)
Bread—and Roses: The Struggle of American Labor, 1865-1915.
Brother, Can You Spare a Dime? The Great Depression: 1929-1933.
Milestones to American Liberty.

Biography

Langston Hughes: A Biography.
Thaddeus Stevens and the Fight for Negro Rights.
A Light in the Dark: The Life of Samuel Gridley Howe.
Tongue of Flame: The Life of Lydia Maria Child.
A Thoreau Profile (with Walter Harding)
Thoreau: People, Principles and Politics.
Mark Twain Himself.
Margaret Sanger: Pioneer of Birth Control (with Lawrence Lader)

Designed by Dick Martin, Chestnut House

ISBN 0 695–80138–4 Trade binding
ISBN 0 695–40138–6 Titan binding

Library of Congress Catalog Card Number: 78–118922

First Printing I

For Medgar Evers

Contents

Foreword

Talk about the South, and Mississippi is on every-body's mind. It is the poorest state in the Union. By almost any standard of life's decencies, it ranks near the bottom. It is hard to forget that fall of 1962 when it took the armed power of the United States to force open the doors of the University of Missis-sippi for a black student named James Meredith. Or that Freedom Summer of 1964 when three young civil rights workers were murdered, eighty were beaten, and dozens of homes and churches were bombed and burned.

Yet freedom *did* come to Mississippi. It was a hundred years ago, and it didn't stay. But out of the blood and wreckage of the Civil War a new life was born to the South. Slavery was ended and four million freedmen, together with the poor whites, tasted democracy for the first time. They voted at last, they built the South's first public school system, they fought to farm their own land, they were elected to local, county, and state offices, and twenty-two of them went to Congress.

This book pictures Reconstruction by offering a close-up of what it was like in Mississippi. Reconstruction was not what most whites, North or South, think it was. They hold to a myth, a nightmare rather, which modern historians have shattered as they seek to establish the truth. Eleven states of the Confederacy came back into the Union after the war, and all went through a reconstruction. The events in each differed in many particulars, but certain developments were basic to all. Mississippi and South Carolina saw the finest flowering of Reconstruction before the era ended. By finding out what happened when freedom came to Mississippi, the reader may understand more easily what happened to the South. And to the nation.

Countless thousands of men and women came out of slavery to battle for civil rights, economic justice, and black power. Many unknowns rose from the ranks to become the leaders of that freedom movement. It happened once, and knowing that it did, many believe it will happen again.

1

No more driver's lash

They swarmed like bees to the honey of freedom. Wherever the Union armies marched that spring of 1863, the slaves rushed to meet them. They poured off the plantations, ragged, feet bleeding, sick, but burning with hope.

The Civil War had been going on for two years. General Grant's armies were pushing down the Mississippi Valley to begin the siege of Vicksburg. At the sound of the guns, many planters deserted their cotton fields and fled before the enemy's

As the Union forces pushed into the South, slaves ran off the plantations by the thousands. They followed in the Army's wake.

approach. As the masters ran in one direction, the slaves ran in the other, proclaiming their own emancipation. Soon there were 50,000 freedmen in the Union camps along the Mississippi. When Vicksburg fell in July, the city became the gate of heaven to the slaves. "They came trooping to it as pigeons to their roost at night," one reporter said. Black cavalrymen raided Jackson, and when they left they were followed by nine-tenths of the city's black population. By the spring of 1865, probably half the blacks of Mississippi had helped themselves to freedom.

It was no different in other parts of the South. In Virginia and the Carolinas, in Kentucky and Arkansas, thousands and thousands of blacks of all ages heard the jubilant liberty bell and came singing to its call.

> No more driver's lash for me
> No more, no more:
> No more driver's lash for me
> Many thousands gone.

The Southern whites had fought the war to preserve and expand slavery. The slave masters thought the only way they could keep their human property was to go out of the Union and set up their own government. The North had gone into the war with the limited view of preserving the Union. But the men and women, black and white, who had worked for a generation to rid the country of the sin of slavery, knew this was wrong. The abolitionists argued that the Union could not win unless the war was fought to end slavery. Frederick Douglass, the powerful voice of black America, said that war carried on to enslave colored men forever "calls logically and loudly for colored men to help suppress it." He urged Lincoln to call both slaves and free Negroes into service to fight in an army of liberation.

Lincoln moved slowly, slowly, toward the Emancipation Proclamation. But on January 1, 1863, he did pronounce the freedom words, and soon after the Union ranks were opened to blacks. By the war's end, 210,000 had served in the Union Army and Navy. A quarter of a million more helped in labor battalions. From Mississippi alone came almost 18,000 blacks to take part in the struggle for their freedom. Their blood mingled with the blood of the 38,000 black men who gave their lives in battle.

It was at Milliken's Bend, a Union fort upstream from Vicksburg, that Mississippi's ex-slaves first met their test of battle. The black volunteers went into action just sixteen days after they were mustered in. They had almost no experience in the use of arms, and the guns they were given were faultily made. With the First Mississippi Regiment holding the center of the line, the Union force of 1100 was attacked by 1500 Texans. A bloody hand-to-hand fight with bayonets and rifle butts took

place in 95 degree heat. The fight lasted all morning, the longest bayonet battle of the war. At noon
a Union warship tipped the scales when it pulled
up in the river and shelled the Confederates' right
flank. The rebels retreated.

The black soldiers lost 39 percent killed or
wounded in one of the toughest encounters of
American military history. "It is impossible for men
to show greater bravery than the Negro troops in
that fight," General Dennis reported. Even the Confederate commander, General McCulloch, had to
pay tribute to the blacks. "The charge was resisted
by the Negro portion of the enemy's force with con-
siderable obstinacy," he wrote, "while the white or
true Yankee portion ran like whipped curs almost
as soon as the charge was ordered."

Near Milliken's Bend were many plantations
from which the owners had fled. The thousands of
slaves left behind were free now, and so were the
thousands more who had flooded into the Union
lines. But what did freedom mean? Was it something
you were told you were, a condition Lincoln's words
put you in? Or was it something you took for your-
self, something you made your own? Many who had
heard they were free proved it by getting up and
walking off the plantation. They left the place of
slavery and left the master who had held them in

bondage. Some went at once, while others finished
the season at their usual labors and then went away.
To come and go as you chose—that was one of freedom's greatest blessings.

Most who left settled not far from the place
where they had been slaves. Many, who had proved
their freedom by departing, came back to work as
freedmen for their old masters. Sometimes they did
this because they could find work no place else. But
sometimes it was simply because they loved the land
they had been born on and worked. It was their
home, too, not just the white man's.

Some of the Mississippi migrants headed for
homes from which they had run away long ago, to
reunite with family. Others hunted for friends or
relatives who had been sold away. But most turned
toward the towns—Natchez, Vicksburg, Jackson,
Columbus, Holly Springs. They could not be called
cities for none had over 7000 population. But slaves
on the remote plantations had longed to see even a
village. Now they could satisfy their curiosity, and
perhaps find work at wages far better than those
paid on the plantations.

Many freedmen, clustered in the towns, were
accused of not wanting to work. It was not that they
wished to be idle. But now they wanted to work for
themselves, when they wanted, and the way they

Slaves leaving their homes to find freedom for themselves.

wanted. After a lifetime of unrewarded labor, was it anything strange? And hardly any of them wanted ever again to cultivate a cotton field. They were eager to plant, but it was food crops they were interested in, crops that would feed their families.

With liberty, came the ability to ignore the endless rules and regulations that had bound them

in slavery. Now they refused to step off the side-
walk for a white—they would not bow; they rode
horses or carriages when they could; they dressed
as they liked; they got dogs and shotguns, and went
hunting just as the whites did.

And talk? To say just what was on your mind, to
speak up in public, to get together in meetings
whenever and wherever you liked—that was freedom! Sometimes they used their liberty to show
their true feelings toward whites, especially their
former masters. They took great pleasure in showing feelings they had been forced to conceal.
"Insolent!" and "Insubordinate!" said many an
angry ex-slaveholder to a once-faithful-and-humble
freedman.

Most of all, what the blacks hoped freedom
would mean was *land*. The great mass of ex-slaves
had spent all their lives working on the master's
land, to provide him with comfort and security.
How could freedom without land be freedom? "Gib
us our own land and we take care ourselves," a reporter heard from freedmen everywhere that spring
of 1865. "But without land, de ole massa can hire
us or starve us, as dey please."

But even before land, there was the need to
stay alive. The refugees in the army camps at
Natchez and Vicksburg were in terrible condition.

One observer wrote they were "crowded together, sickly, disheartened, dying on the streets, not a family of them all either well-sheltered, clad, or fed; no physician, no medicine, no hospitals."

General Grant set up contraband camps or freedmen's villages. He gave them tents, rations, and medical aid. The blacks were put to work for wages on the abandoned cotton fields. Local whites were angry, they tried to stop production, stealing stock and wrecking equipment. Bands of Confederate guerrillas attacked the workers in the fields. Nevertheless, a lot of cotton was ginned and sold for the benefit of the federal government.

It was a kind of communal enterprise with the government as sponsor. It could have turned into a large-scale system of producing cotton. But the general in command of the project decided to drop it. Instead, he turned the abandoned plantations over to whites, who leased them for next to nothing. They used the equipment, the horses and mules, and paid the freedmen only a few dollars a month to do the work.

The freedmen were given food and shelter, but had to pay for their clothing and other supplies. The landlords were as careless of the black's rights as any slaveowner. Many made handsome profits out of their favorable contracts. The farm workers lived in shacks, suffered from overcrowding, and disease, and wound up with little or no pay. Out of these earnings, too, a tax was taken to pay for the support of dependents.

To every Northerner who came South, local whites repeated over and over again two standard charges against the blacks: they wouldn't work and they were dishonest.

When the reporter Whitelaw Reid heard this all over Georgia, he noted, "I have found no Georgian who, now that his slaves can no longer be made to work for him, expects to work for himself. In fact, working for themselves does not seem to be a part of their philosophy of life. Work is for 'niggers'— not for white men."

Visiting Alabama, Reid discovered that the army had issued rations to destitute people in Mobile, black and white. He checked the official records and found that in June, 1865, the white "master race" had drawn ten times as many rations as the blacks had requested:

A stranger might have concluded that it was the white race that was going to prove unable to take care of itself, instead of the emancipated slaves, over whose future, unless brightened by some vision of compulsory labor, their late loving masters grew so sad.

The explanation was a simple one. The Negroes had gone to work: it was the only way they knew for getting bread. . . . The whites had nobody left to go to work for them, and that was the only way to get bread *they* knew.

Another reporter who went South, Thomas W. Knox of the New York *Herald,* also heard many whites say blacks were shiftless and dishonest. He studied the complaints and wrote:

There can be no effect without a cause. . . . The system of slavery necessitated a constant struggle between the slave and his overseer. It was the duty of the latter to obtain the greatest amount of labor from the sinews of the slave. It was the business of the slave to perform as little labor as possible. It made no difference to him whether the plantation produced a hundred or a thousand bales. He received nothing beyond his subsistence and clothing. His labor had no compensation, and his balance sheet at the end of the month, or year, was the same, whether he had been idle or industrious. It was plainly to his personal interest to do nothing he could in any way avoid. The Negro displayed his sagacity by deceiving the overseer whenever he could do so. The best white man in the world would have shunned all labor under such circumstances. The

Negro evinced a pardonable weakness in pretending to be ill whenever he could hope to make the pretense successful.

Getting no pay for his labor, the slave naturally tried to compensate himself. He liked roasted pork, for instance, but that article didn't appear on plantation rations. So he might grab a fatted pig when he thought the chance of being caught was small. One freedman explained to Knox how he used to look upon stealing one of master's hogs:

You see, master owns his saddle-horse, and he owns lots of corn. Master would be very mad if I didn't give the horse all the corn he wanted. Now, he owns me, and he owns a great many hogs. I like hogs, just as much as the horse likes corn, but when master catches me killing the hogs he is very mad, and he makes the overseer whip me.

In nine cases out of ten, Knox believed, the petty thefts were designed to supply personal wants, rather than for any other purpose. It was usually food that was stolen.

How virtuous were the whites? Colonel Thomas, reporting on the fate of freedmen in Mississippi, said two-thirds of the laborers had been cheated out of their earnings in that first year of liberation. "Honesty," wrote another observer, J.T.

Trowbridge, "appears to be a virtue to be exercised only towards white people: it was too good to be thrown away on niggers."

Much of the help offered the freedmen in the closing years of the war came from friends in the North. Freedmen's aid societies sprang up and sent money, clothing, food, medical supplies. The health services and hospitals were never enough to meet the need. The death rate was very high in the freedmen's camps and even higher on the plantations, where sometimes over half the workers died. Many orphans were left, with few places to care for them.

Families, never a legal unit under slavery, were recognized for the first time. In the army posts thousands of marriages were performed. To the ex-slaves, who had been forcibly separated from husbands, wives, and children, it was another great sign of what freedom meant. So, too, was the important matter of choosing a new family name, a name that became the badge of freedom.

2

The in-between time

When the war ended, much of Mississippi looked as barren as the craters of the moon. Almost every home in the state mourned for some member of the family who had been killed. A traveler who went to a town meeting of three hundred in Aberdeen said a third of the people had lost an arm or a leg, and half the rest showed other signs of war injuries. In some places he saw only women and children and old men. Where there had once been shops and stores and warehouses, now there were heaps of ruins.

The farmlands had gone to waste. Fences had been trampled down by the contending armies or had collapsed from neglect. Weeds and bushes crept over the fields. The tools to farm were ruined or missing; many of the farm animals were gone. Banks were locked, businesses shut tight. The railways were torn up, printing presses wrecked. It was hard to know what was going on anywhere in the state, or outside it, for the postal system was crippled, and only a few newspapers still managed to appear.

A hundred years before the war the Mississippi Territory held hardly 500 blacks and whites. It was during the Revolution that many rich Tories, supporters of the British, fled the rebel colonies to take up the best of this dark western land and establish plantations. To the penniless adventurers were left the poorer pine uplands.

With the plantation system, came slavery. Wherever the soil was suitable, the newcomers started raising staple crops with black slave labor. In 1817, the territory became the state of Mississippi.

When the state joined the Confederacy in 1861, the population was 790,000. There were more blacks than whites—437,000 slaves to 354,000 whites. Most of the whites were not slaveowners. Only 30,000 had slaves, and of these about 6000 were the big slaveholders.

The great majority of slaves were on the plantations. In some cotton counties there were more than ten blacks to each white. Most of the slaves of working age were field hands. They were taught little more than the simple tasks of growing crops. They were forbidden to learn to read and write. A few were given special training as house servants, craftsmen, or mechanics. Some, who worked in the small towns, were able to learn more.

How hard did slaves work on a plantation? J. T. Trowbridge, who talked with many planters at the end of the war, asked what the hours were on a well-run Mississippi plantation. This is the answer he got:

Mr. P——'s niggers were in the field at daylight. It was so in the longest days of summer, as at other times of the year. They worked till six o'clock, when their breakfast was carried to them. They had just time enough allowed them to eat their breakfast; then they worked till noon, when their dinner was carried to them. They had an hour for their dinner. At six o'clock their supper was carried to them. Then they worked till dark. There were cisterns in the field, where they got their water. Nobody was allowed to leave the field from the time they entered it in the morning until work was over at night. That was to save time. The women who suckled babies had their babies carried to them. A little nigger-boy used to drive a mule to the field with a cart full of nigger babies; and the women gave their brats their luncheon while they ate their own. So not a minute was lost.

This was a "liberal" Mississippian's plantation, managed by a "considerate and merciful overseer." The slaves put in a 16-hour day in summer, and more, for they all had chores to do when they got home after dark.

There were only 775 free blacks, and most of these made their living doing odd jobs in the towns. There were never many free blacks because after 1842 a state law made it impossible for anyone to free slaves in his will. Nowhere in the state were free blacks welcome. State and local law and custom cramped and confined their freedom. Many times they were pressured to move to other states or to go to Africa.

No matter what their condition, black men woke up every morning with their minds on freedom. And then it came on the Union army's bayonets:

> Slavery chain done broke at last, broke at last,
>   broke at last,
> Slavery chain done broke at last,
> Going to praise God till I die.

Most of the white Southerners could not think of blacks as anything but slaves. Whites believed blacks were a separate and inferior race of mankind and were their property by natural right. The Confederates knew they had lost the war, of course, and losing it, had lost slavery, too. But "they still have an ingrained feeling that the blacks at large belong to the whites at large," said Carl Schurz, who traveled through the South right after the war to investigate conditions for President Andrew Johnson.

When Schurz reached Mississippi, he learned the ex-Confederates had organized county patrols to keep the blacks in slavery. In many cases, freedmen who had gone looking for their wives and children on the plantations were driven off and told they could not have them. In other places, he was told, "the blacks are in a much worse state than ever before, the able-bodied being kept at work under the lash, and the young and infirm driven off to care for themselves. As to protection from the civil authorities, there is no such thing . . ."

Along the Mississippi, north of Natchez, the laborers suffered from lack of food and clothing. Planters kept supplies low because they feared to lose them to the raiding Confederate guerrillas. On many plantations in the lower river valley the whipping of freedmen was common. Native white overseers especially seemed to itch to give blows and kicks. The old slave system had not passed for them.

How the guerrillas operated was described by Thomas Knox, the *Herald's* correspondent. Near the war's end he leased a cotton plantation along the Mississippi. While visiting Natchez one day, news came that the guerrillas had raided his plantation. He rushed back and learned that thirty men had surrounded his house and broken in with pistols ready to kill him. Failing to find him, they captured his overseer as he was trying to escape. The freedmen were plowing in the fields at the time, and those who could, loosened the mules from the plows, mounted them, and fled.

Nineteen blacks, ten of them children, were captured and carried off. A sixty-five-year-old woman fell exhausted after being marched three miles. She was beaten senseless and left by the roadside. Except for a few blacks who escaped along the way, the rest were sold into slavery. Four days later Knox found his overseer in the woods nearby, shot through the head. His body had been stripped of all his clothing. Knox had to abandon the plantation.

Many of the neighboring plantations were given up for the same cause. Knox reported that when the guerrillas captured two men who had leased a plantation near Vicksburg, they tortured them before putting them to death. They cut off the ears of one man and broke his nose with a blow from a club. Then they tied him to a tree and auctioned off the privilege of shooting him. His partner was forced to watch the mutilation and murder, then was made to dig his own grave, and shot as he stood at the edge.

The guerrillas were determined that Yankees, or men who stayed home and were friendly with the Yankees, shouldn't make money out of the cotton plantations.

General Chetlain, in command for two months of the nine-county region around Jackson, reported an average of one black man killed every day. When he rode forty miles out from his base he found "seven Negroes brutally butchered." Black soldiers were the special target of the killers.

Mr. Yancey, a wealthy planter living in De Soto County, wrote General Fisk: "As to recognizing the rights of freedmen to their children, I will say there is not one man or woman in the South who believes they are free. . . . We consider them as stolen property of the damnable United States government."

Another planter told General Fisk he hoped and expected slavery would be restored in some form. One visitor in Mississippi wrote Senator Charles Sumner to say that the old overseers were in power again. "The object of the Southerners appears to be to make good their often repeated assertions, to the effect that the Negroes would die if they were freed. To make it so, they seem determined to goad them to desperation, in order to have an excuse to turn upon and annihilate them."

Voices in the North spoke up in protest. Had all this blood been shed to leave the freedmen in the hands of their former masters?

In March, 1865, Congress acted. It set up a Freedmen's Bureau and put it under the wing of the War Department. The Bureau was to provide food, clothing, and medical care for the needy, white or black. It was to settle the freedmen on the abandoned lands. It was to help them find work, aid them in their dealings with the planters, and open up schools for them.

The office of a Freedmen's Bureau, where the ex-slaves could get advice, help, or a hearing.

In Mississippi, the Bureau divided the state into several districts. It put officers of black regiments in charge. By December, 1865, there were fifty-eight local agents and sixty-seven teachers working for the Bureau, a number that grew until the agency closed down in 1869.

The agents moved out from headquarters to talk to the freedmen in the towns and on the plantations. The first thing they did was to tell them they were free, legally free, now and forever. For there were many whites who kept saying the blacks were not free, and some, on the remote plantations, who kept the news of freedom from their slaves.

The agents printed circulars about the freedmen's rights and asked the black ministers to read them to their congregations. They also gave the circulars to the planters so they would know the policies and rules of the Freedmen's Bureau. They did all they could to win the cooperation of all the people.

The emergency food relief the Bureau was allotted for Mississippi did not amount to very much. About 3000 blacks (out of 400,000) got rations each month in the fall of 1865. By winter, the number dropped to 570, and stayed around there through the next two years. Bad crops in the winter of 1867-68 led to mass hunger. Congress approved increased rations to prevent starvation. But a good policy can easily be abused when it is in the hands of an executive opposed to it. In Mississippi the Bureau chief was General Alvin C.

The freedmen who left the plantations built villages such as this on the edge of the cities.

Gillem, a Southern Democrat appointed by President Johnson. His sympathies were entirely with the planters. He believed food relief would encourage the blacks to be idle and make them feel independent so he cut it down even more. Many planters were pleased, for it meant blacks would be

willing to work for less, or for nothing but food. No
wonder this general became popular with the
whites and hated by the blacks.

To care for sick freedmen, the Bureau opened
hospitals in the towns. They were really only
places where medicine was handed out, and most
closed in less than a year. But they helped by teaching the freedmen better health practices.

The Bureau's goal was to end relief as soon as
possible. It encouraged blacks to find work and
watched to see that contracts for labor were carried
out by both parties. When the freedmen brought
in complaints, the Bureau gave advice and tried to
protect them from abuses. It got lawyers to help
them prepare their cases. It forced the state to accept their testimony in the courts.

Dead set against any organization that would
help the blacks, the planters hated the Bureau from
the start. A newspaper in Panola County probably
spoke for most white Mississippians when it ran
these lines on its front pages for several months:

> Breathes there a man with soul so dead,
> Who never to himself hath said,
> G-d d-n the Freemen's Bureau.

The whites said the Bureau meddled in matters
that were none of its business. They said it gave

the blacks false hopes and made them discontented. They said its agents were not fit or were dishonest. True, some agents were anxious to please the whites among whom they were living. They accepted the planters' belief that blacks were lazy and inferior people who needed to be forced to work. There were agents who took bribes or neglected their work.

But the fact was, the freedmen wanted land, and education, and civil rights, and the ballot. And anyone who encouraged them in their demands was naturally no friend of the planters.

3

Which way
to go?

Just how free was the freedman to be?

This question became one of the big political
issues long before the Civil War ended. Everyone
knew how the white South felt. The new governor
of Mississippi, General Benjamin G. Humphreys,
put it clearly: "It should never be forgotten that
ours is and it shall ever be a government of white
men." The freedmen, he said, "cannot be admitted
to political or social equality with the white race."

How Northerners felt was pretty clear, too. Few in the North were willing to accept full equality between black and white. Most Northern whites, like Southern whites, believed the black was inferior to the white. There were many state laws that enforced racial discrimination. In the election of 1865, the voters of Connecticut, Wisconsin, and Minnesota refused to grant blacks the ballot.

Yet almost everyone agreed that freedom alone was not enough for the ex-slave. He needed immediate help to survive in the war-torn South. He needed to build a new way of life in place of slavery. He needed protection against any attempt of the white South to reenslave him or to force him into some new form of servitude.

The blacks knew what they needed. Frederick Douglass said it plainly in 1865: "I am for the immediate, unconditional, and universal enfranchisement of the black man, in every state in the Union." Without the right to vote, he said, "liberty is a mockery."

Douglass said his people were not looking for charity: "What I ask for the Negro is not benevolence, not pity, not sympathy, but simply *justice.*"

Everybody was asking, as the war ended, "What shall we do with the Negro?"

Said Douglass: "I have had but one answer

Frederick Douglass, who fought for land and full citizenship for the freedmen.

from the beginning. Do nothing with us! All I ask is, give him a chance to stand on his own legs! If you will only untie his hands, and give him a chance, I think he will live. He will work as readily for himself as the white man."

What to do with the old Southern rulers was the other half of the question. They had been defeated. Should they be kept from returning to power? Should their great plantations be taken away? Should the common people, black and white, be given a chance to govern themselves?

No one had a blueprint for what to do. Great upheavals such as the Civil War do not occur according to plan. But early in the war there were men and women who knew how it might end. They were the abolitionists, the blacks and whites who had struggled a long time to end slavery. When they saw the war was going to achieve their goal, they outlined a program. They were the first to urge Lincoln to issue the Emancipation Proclamation. They were the first to call for arming the blacks. They were the first to ask for a Freedmen's Bureau. And now, with the war ended, they said the freedmen should have civil and political equality and land to make themselves independent.

Whatever happened during and after the war was of course not solely the abolitionists' doing.

They did not create events or control them. They were like guides going out in advance of the main body, scouting the terrain for natural dangers and human enemies, and advising those in command how to avoid or overcome them. More, they had a conscience, a sense of this country's promise and possibilities. Their purpose was to extend the blessings of liberty to all, to nurture it everywhere, and to protect it against all enemies.

The debate over Reconstruction began early in the war, as soon as the first Confederate state (Louisiana) was captured by the Union forces. What to do with the defeated state? No states had ever gone out of the Union before this time. There was no history, no precedent, to go by. The Constitution had nothing to say about this problem.

What people do in such circumstances depends on what their political aims are. They take whatever action will carry out their desires, and develop a theory to suit it.

The abolitionists wanted to rebuild the South. They wanted to make it truly democratic. They didn't believe the old planters, used to the ways of slave rule, could ever be won to democracy. Who else could govern, then? There was no middle class in the South—only a small number of merchants and manufacturers and professionals. There were many small farmers, some of them owners and some tenants. White though they were, they had been given second-class treatment all along. Many had opposed disunion, and large numbers had deserted from the Confederate Army. They were hungry for more land, and better land. They wanted a voice in government, too, and a chance to take office. They could help remake the South.

There were not many industrial workers. Factories were few in this agricultural society. Probably there were more skilled workers among the slaves than the whites. So this group was too small and scattered to be of much help in reshaping the old life.

No, the engine power for Reconstruction had to come from the blacks. Their four millions would be the heart of the new democracy. Thousands of new revolutionaries like the Gabriels and Denmark Veseys and Nat Turners of slavery times had fused into a powerful black fist to help crush their oppressors. Yesterday they had been slaves; today they were free men, with guns.

And they were pushing ahead, demanding political rights, demanding land. The Union, they said, must be reconstructed with full political and civil rights guaranteed to all. They did not want to return to the old Union, when free blacks were treated like second-class citizens everywhere.

A bitter struggle developed over Reconstruction. On one side were the abolitionists and their friends in the Republican Party. This wing of Lincoln's party was called the Radical Republicans. They wanted to rebuild the South on a new basis. They believed the Confederate states had given up all their constitutional rights. Defeated now, they should come back into the Union only under conditions laid down by Congress.

The leading spokesmen for the Radicals in Congress were Representative Thaddeus Stevens of Pennsylvania, and Senator Charles Sumner of Massachusetts. Both had been abolitionists long before the war. Both were close allies of such black leaders as Douglass.

Stevens was a tall man who limped about on a cane because of his clubfoot. His brilliance at law earned him wealth, but he always stood on the side of the common man. He fought for free public schools and for free speech for dissenters, and defended fugitive slaves in the courts. "No man was more forthright an advocate of complete democracy for the Negro," said the historian W. E. B. DuBois.

When the Civil War came, Stevens was an old man in his seventies, feeble in body but a fearless leader whose political skill and merciless wit dom-

Charles Sumner, the Massachusetts abolitionist who championed the freedmen's rights in the Senate throughout Reconstruction.

inated the Congress. The mechanic, the farmer, the soldier, the laborer looked to Stevens as their champion. They called him "The Great Commoner."

Sumner was the teammate of Stevens in the Senate. Like Stevens, he was an old anti-slavery fighter. But in style and temperament the two champions were very different. Where Stevens was careless how he looked, Sumner was always handsomely polished. Stevens' wit slashed swiftly to the heart of the argument; Sumner was wordy and high-flown. Stevens was the practical politician who measured the realities and took what he could get. Sumner was the idealist who hated compromise. Once, when Stevens thought Sumner was being impossibly self-righteous in congressional debate, the old man said, "I shall not be driven by clamor or denunciation to throw away a great good because it is not perfect. I will take all I can get in the cause of humanity and leave it to be perfected by better men in better times."

The two Radical leaders clashed with Lincoln over Reconstruction policy. He wanted to restore the old relations between the South and the Union. Except for slavery, he wanted to bring things around to where they had been. And he thought it was the President's duty to decide what conditions the states must meet to return to the Union.

Thaddeus Stevens of Pennsylvania was the leading spokesman for Radical Reconstruction in Congress.

Lincoln showed his hand when he set Reconstruction policy for the first defeated state, Louisiana. He offered full pardon to all but a few of the
Confederates. They need only swear to uphold the
Constitution and respect the Emancipation Proclamation. As soon as a tenth of those who had voted
in 1860 had taken the oath, they could set up a state
government. But it would be for whites only.
Lincoln's plan barred all blacks from taking the
oath, from voting, and from holding office.

Lincoln, it should be remembered, had little
faith in a future for the freedmen in this country.
During the war he kept proposing that the blacks
should be helped out of the country to set up colonies somewhere overseas.

The angry blacks in Louisiana sent a delegation
to protest to Lincoln. He then wrote privately to
Louisiana's governor, suggesting the educated
blacks, and those who had fought for the Union,
should be permitted to vote. But the state's whites
paid no attention. Then Tennessee and Arkansas
moved to reconstruct. They did the same thing,
refusing to let blacks vote.

The Radicals kept pressing hard. They feared
the Emancipation Proclamation, a war measure,
might not be recognized by a peacetime government. To make sure it would stick, and apply na-
tionwide, they campaigned for a constitutional

amendment. On January 31, 1865, the final vote was taken in the House. The Thirteenth Amendment, which brought an end to human bondage in the United States, passed with just two votes to spare. The long years of struggle by black and white abolitionists had triumphed.

Hardly two months later, the war was over, and Lincoln was killed by an assassin's bullet. Now the Radicals had to deal with the Tennessean who took Lincoln's place in the White House.

Andrew Johnson was a poor white, a tailor who educated himself. He had risen in Democratic politics from congressman to governor to senator. Himself the owner of eight slaves, he yet voted against the extension of slavery and opposed secession. He stayed with the Union when the fighting started, becoming governor of Tennessee. Johnson helped the poor farmers by backing the Homestead Act, which gave them free Western lands. But he was against dividing the abandoned plantations among the poor whites in his own state.

In 1864, Lincoln had feared he would not be reelected unless he could win some votes from those Democrats who supported the Union, like Johnson. So he made the Tennessean his running mate. Thad Stevens had warned Lincoln it was a mistake. "Andrew Johnson is a rank demagogue," he said, "and I suspect at heart a damned scoundrel."

A month after Lincoln's death Stevens called on Johnson to see what his plans for Reconstruction were. Congress was not in session and would not meet again until December. Stevens said he didn't think the President had the constitutional power to carry out Reconstruction alone. He suggested Johnson suspend plans until Congress could meet.

But Johnson didn't listen. He wanted to get his own program going right away, without interference from Stevens and Sumner.

Seeing what was happening, the Southern planters didn't sit by idly. They rushed up to Washington that spring. With their aristocratic ladies, they came to call at the White House. Johnson, always envious of the gentry, was a natural target for their flattery. They begged him to be generous with the rebel leaders. They invited him to return to the Democratic Party.

Many abolitionists, at the same time, hoped that Johnson would be more radical than Lincoln. So they courted the President too. Johnson was polite to all; it was hard to tell what he really thought.

Then one day he spoke, and acted. And everyone knew where he was headed.

What happened in Mississippi tells the story.

4

White governors, black codes

The trouble began in the late spring of 1865. President Johnson proclaimed pardon to almost all ex-Confederates. They would get their property back, he said, except for slaves. It meant the plantation owners could keep all their vast lands.

On the same day, he ruled that when a majority of a Confederate state's *white* voters had taken a loyalty oath, they could form a new constitution and bring the state back into the Union.

A few days later, he appointed William Sharkey provisional governor of Mississippi. Sharkey had been an important slaveholder before the war. For a long time he had been chief justice of the state's highest court.

The ex-Confederates were delighted. Johnson was their friend. He was being even more generous with them than Lincoln. This was their chance to return to power.

Sharkey announced an election in August for delegates to a constitutional convention. Only those who had been voters as of January, 1861, could take part—which ruled out blacks. Next, he reappointed all local officials who had been holding the jobs under the Confederacy. Again—whites only. Finally, he urged President Johnson to withdraw all federal troops from the state—blacks, mostly. (Within a year, Johnson had removed all the 9000 soldiers, except for a single battalion of white infantry.)

The blacks were angry and bitter. In Vicksburg they held a mass meeting. Jacob Richardson, a soldier of the Forty-ninth U.S. Colored Infantry, presided. They protested loudly to President Johnson. How could he permit Mississippi to call a convention and hold an election, with only whites allowed to vote? What kind of democracy was

This cartoon from the Northern press supported the use of federal troops to protect the freedmen from white racists.

that? Was this what the war had been fought for?
They demanded the right to vote for *all*, regardless
of race.

But Mississippi went right ahead. The old
rulers were back in control. They held an all-white
convention that drew up a new state constitution.
Every delegate was dead set against political rights
in any form for the blacks. They did nothing for the
freedmen. They even refused to adopt the Thirteenth Amendment. Instead, they abolished slavery
in such a loose way that an opening was left for it to
return.

Again Vicksburg blacks met, this time to protest
the work of the convention. The planters mean to
put us back into slavery, they warned.

It was an uncertain summer. There was no au-
thority in the state. It had a temporary governor, a
new constitution, and no legislature. Power was
really in the hands of federal troops, who occupied
the state. But they, too, had no clear sense of what
their function was. The President said they were
there to aid but not to interfere with the provisional
government. Neither Johnson nor the War Department told them exactly what they should do about
the reconstruction process.

Yet the Freedmen's Bureau was on the scene,
too, with a military organization, and its purpose

was to help the blacks take the steps from slavery
to freedom.

Governor Sharkey and the white leaders didn't
think that the blacks needed any such help. They
feared military power would back up the freedmen's
demand for political power.

That summer disorders erupted in many parts
of the state. Mississippi was really frontier country;
lawbreakers and desperadoes were common before
the war. Now gangs of lawless whites operated
everywhere in the interior. One of the President's
observers, Benjamin G. Truman, reported that "Mississippians have been shooting and cutting each
other all over the State, to a greater extent than in all
the other states of the Union put together . . . I
read of shooting and cutting in every little paper I
pick up, while I have seen more of it in the last
few days than I saw in New York in six years." In
his diary, Judge Jason Niles wrote that violence re-
sulting in death was an everyday happening in
central Mississippi where he lived.

The army units were not stationed in every
county, but only near the bigger towns. Many of
the troops were black. The whites were not used to
being ordered about by blacks; they hated it. Ten-
sion built up. Their feelings were voiced by a newspaper editorial:

Our citizens, who had been accustomed to meet and
treat the Negroes only as respectful servants, were
mortified, pained, and shocked to encounter them in
towns and villages, and on the public roads, by scores
and hundreds and thousands, wearing Federal uni-
forms, and bearing bright muskets and gleaming bayonets. They often recognized among them those who had
once been their own servants. . . . Their hearts sick-
ened. . . . when they saw their own slaves freed, armed,
and put on guard over them.

The black troops, some of whom were from the
North, were friendly to the freedmen, and encouraged their struggle for equal rights. The black
soldiers were disciplined and committed no offenses
against the native whites. But even when they kept
order, the planters claimed their presence "demoral-
ized" the blacks.

The planters began to clamor for their own
armed forces. Sharkey let the counties organize
militia companies "to prevent crime." Only whites
were allowed in. Most of them were former rebel
soldiers, and they continued to wear their Confederate gray. They used terror against any freedmen
who showed any sign of independence.

At once the federal commander in the state
ordered Sharkey to drop the militia. Sharkey ap-
pealed over his head to the President.

On Johnson's desk lay reports from the military, from the press, and from teachers, of whippings, shootings, lynchings, not only in Mississippi but throughout the South. On top was the letter from Carl Schurz, telling him that the militia patrols "indulged in the gratification of private vengeance, persecuted helpless Union people and freedmen, and endeavored to keep the plantation Negroes in a state of virtual slavery."

Nevertheless, Johnson overruled his general and let the rebel militia units go on. Nothing he had done so far aroused more distrust in the North.

That fall the first postwar legislature was elected in Mississippi. Under the new state constitution, only whites voted and only whites were elected. The same situation held all over the South. Blacks were thought not fit to vote and not fit to hold office. Ex-Confederates were elected wholesale to local and state office, as well as to Congress.

The first business of the Mississippi legislature was the freedman. The planters wanted to assure a stable and cheap labor supply, and they wanted to fix the black man in his place in Mississippi life. Local newspaper editors set the tone for the session. The Canton *American Citizen* demanded laws that would "compel the negroes to work as formerly upon the plantations . . . willingly, if possible, but forcibly, if need be." The Jackson *News* advised that the Negro "be kept in the position which God almighty intended him to occupy; *a position inferior to the white man.*"

Humphreys, the new governor, echoed this when he said, "Ours is and it shall ever be, a government of white men."

The legislature made it clear at once what that meant to the freedman. It adopted what was called the Black Code of 1865. It was the first set of such laws regulating the life and labor of the freedman to be passed in many Southern states after the war. The black codes showed what the ex-Confederates wanted the place of the freedman to be.

The freedman was denied the right to live in a town without permission from the town authorities.

He could not testify in court against a white man, or sit on a grand or a petit jury. He could be whipped by the court, by the "master," "mistress," employer, or overseer.

He could not own a farm. He could rent or lease land only in the towns.

The freedman's labor was closely regulated. He had to show a license from police or a written labor contract to prove employment. Any contract he made for his labor must be witnessed by two whites. If he quit a job before his contract was up, he could be arrested by anyone and returned to his employer. If he had no job, he could be picked up as a vagrant and hired off to any planter who would pay his fine. If he had money enough to pay the fine himself, he was still considered a vagrant and could be again arrested, tried, found guilty, and again fined. Until, presumably, he either consented to a contract or, penniless, was auctioned off to a planter.

A freedman's children could be forced into apprenticeship if he was unable to provide for them. Former owners were given first choice of such children.

A freedman could not ride in first class railroad cars used by whites.

He could not bear arms.

He could be fined or jailed for "seditious speeches, insulting gestures, language or acts."

He was forbidden to assemble with other freedmen in any number greater than five, "at any place of public resort, or at any meetinghouse or houses in the night, or at any school for teaching them reading or writing, either in the daytime or night." Violation of this part of the code was punishable by "thirty-nine lashes on the bare back."

The right to vote? The code didn't mention it.

The freedman could have legal marriage and

children. But he was forbidden to marry with any
white person. If he did, it was a felony punishable
by life imprisonment.

A white who married a black was liable to the
same life penalty. A white also faced fine and imprisonment if he was found "unlawfully assembling"
or "usually associating" with a freedman on terms
of "equality," or if he sold, loaned, or gave a black
food, shelter, or clothing when the black was escaping from his employer, or if he tried to persuade
a black to leave his employer.

As for laws, Mississippi simply put her old
slave code back into effect. All the penal and crim-
inal laws that applied to the slave were given full
force and effect against the freedman, except for
some changes in the mode and manner of trial and
imprisonment.

What was the effect of the Black Code?

One observer, A. T. Morgan, a Union colonel
now making his home in the state, said:

In the county Yazoo, under these provisions, men and
women were cheated, swindled, robbed, whipped,
hunted with bloodhounds, shot, killed; nay, more, men
were robbed of their wives, their children, their sweet-
hearts; fathers, brothers, sons, saw their mothers, wives,
sisters, seduced, betrayed, raped, and if Yazoo *law* af-

forded them any promise of redress, Yazoo *practice* gave
them no remedy whatever.

The freedmen were very reluctant to hire their
labor to the planters under the harsh code, especially in the interior of Mississippi, away from the
towns and the federal militia. As the season for beginning the year's cotton work was rapidly passing,
the planters became anxious. They even tried kind
manners when they approached a freedman, but he
usually shied away. One old Mississippian, desper-
ate for field hands, went to New Orleans to hunt for
some, and returned in a great rage. He told Whitelaw Reid:

Do you believe, sah, I even demeaned myself so much
as to go to a damned nigger, who called himself a labor
agent, and offered him five dollars a head for all the
hands he could get me. He promised 'em at once, and I
was all right till I told him they was to be sent to Mississippi. To think of it, sah! The black scoundrel told
me flat he wouldn't send a man. "Why not," says I;
"I'll give you your money when they start." "I wouldn't
send you a man ef you gave me a hundred dollars a
head," said the dirty, impudent black dog. And why?
All because the sassy scoundrel said he didn't like our
Mississippi laws.

The Cincinnati *Enquirer* reported that the President was supposed to have said to the governor of Missouri, "This is a country for white men, and by God, so long as I am President, it shall be a government for white men." The Jackson *News* in Mississippi promptly printed at its masthead: "This is a white man's country—President Johnson."

There were some native whites who thought the legislators had gone much too far with the Black Code. One editor said the legislators were "a set of men who seem bent on following the dictates of every blind prejudice, let the consequences be ever so ruinous to the State and the people."

"One is amazed at such stupidity," said J. H. Jones, a Confederate colonel. "The fortunes of the whole South have been injured by their folly," said the Columbus *Sentinel*.

One of the first attacks on the Black Code came from the freedmen themselves. They held a convention in Vicksburg. They sent an angry petition to President Johnson demanding he throw out the Black Code. If it is allowed to go into effect, they said, "It will be virtually returning us to slavery again. To this we will not submit in any form, and you may know what that means."

Johnson's reply? A few weeks later, in a message to the Senate, he spoke of the Black Codes as "measures to confer upon freedmen the privileges which are essential to their comfort, protection, and security."

The Radical Republicans refused to accept that. They would not stand by while the landlords forged new chains for black laborers. The *Chicago Tribune* said, "We will tell the white men of Mississippi that the men of the North will convert the state of Mississippi into a frog pond before they will allow such laws to disgrace one foot of soil in which the bones of our soldiers sleep and over which the flag of freedom waves."

Stevens worked out a plan to stop the Johnson reconstruction. The Congress set up a Committee of Fifteen to form a new policy.

Early in 1866 the Committee brought scores of witnesses to Washington. They testified on life in the South. People of all points of view, North and South, black and white, had their say. At the end, 700 pages of printed testimony were piled high. It added up to this:

There was still strong hatred for the Union in the South. Southern whites who had opposed secession were treated like enemies. The feeling against the blacks was worse than before the war. The army and the Freedmen's Bureau were needed to provide protection. State elections could not be accepted as

valid. The states could not be allowed to play a part
in the Union again until they guaranteed the civil
rights of all their citizens. It was "madness and
lunacy," the Committee concluded, for the President
to hand so much power to the Confederates.

Congress then got down to passing bills for a
sound reconstruction program. First it resolved that
no state could be restored until Congress approved
it. This took away Johnson's emergency powers
and made Congress supreme in this matter.

Then it continued the Freedmen's Bureau for
another year, and increased its powers. And finally,
it put through a civil rights bill guaranteeing the
four million freedmen equality before the law.

Johnson vetoed both the Civil Rights and the
Freedmen's Bureau bills. But Stevens mustered the
two-thirds majority of Congress needed to override
the President.

Now the blacks would have a real chance to
test freedom.

5

Forty acres and a mule

Early in 1863 Union cavalrymen raided the country-side around Jackson, Mississippi. They carried the news of emancipation to the slaves on a big plantation. "You're free! You're free!" they cried, as they gave the blacks guns, and rode off. At once the freedmen took a plowline and measured off the land. They divided it fairly among themselves, and then, dividing the farm tools, too, they set to work on their own land.

The one-farm revolution didn't last long.

Soon Confederate soldiers moved in. They captured the blacks and put them in jail in Jackson.

The local paper, the *Mississippian,* was furious at what the blacks had dared to do. The same thing had taken place wherever Union troops invaded plantation territory in the South. See what happens? the editor warned his readers. If the Federals win, "Lincoln's robbers will occupy every farm in the South."

Many Southern papers were sounding the same warning. They believed a victory for the North would mean the plantations would be taken away and handed over to the slaves.

The slaves believed it, too. It was a feeling deep in their bones. They knew this land, they had tilled it for generations. Their unpaid labor had made the planters prosperous. If justice meant anything, it meant they would receive at least a part of this land they had bought and paid for by their sweat and blood.

Almost from the beginning of the war, the question of land for the freed slaves had been debated. Some proposed paying the slave owners for their land. To that, John Rock, a black lawyer in Boston, answered:

Why talk of compensating masters? Compensate them them for what? What do you owe them? What does the slave owe them? What does society owe them? Compensate the master? It is the slave who ought to be compensated. The property of the South is by right the property of the slave. You talk of compensating the master who has stolen enough to sink ten generations, and yet you do not propose to restore even a part of that which has been plundered. Restore to the freedman the wealth of the South. This you owe to the slave; and if you do your duty, posterity will give to you the honor of being the first nation that dared to deal justly by the oppressed.

Prince Rivers, a black sergeant in the First South Carolina Volunteers, put it directly: "Every colored man will be a slave, and feel himself a slave, until he can raise him own bale of cotton and put him own mark upon it and say dis is mine!"

The abolitionists said again and again a new life for the freedmen needed the solid base of economic independence. If the black had no land of his own, the white planter would still be able to treat him like a slave.

Where was the land to come from?

Break up the big plantations, said the abolitionists. Parcel them out to the landless farmer, black and white.

This will bring two great benefits, they pointed out. With the economic power of the planters cut away, the South will become more democratic. And the ex-slaves and poor whites will gain a greater voice in political life. This new class of small land-owners will be loyal to the government that has given them a fresh start in life.

Early in the war, Congress passed a mild confiscation bill. It would take away from the rebels only that property (including slaves) which was used to help the Confederate war effort.

The abolitionists were not satisfied. Everywhere in the world, they said, those who rebelled against their government paid with their property —and often their lives—if they lost. It was a custom all civilized nations accepted. When the Tories who refused to support the American Revolution were driven into Canada, their property had been taken over by the new American republic. And it had never been given back.

The argument convinced many. Another, stronger Confiscation Act was passed by Congress. It would take all the property belonging to the rebels as well as freeing all their slaves.

But Lincoln strongly opposed it. He said he would veto the bill, unless it was toned down. He did not think the sons and daughters of a rebel should have to pay for their father's wrongdoing. So the Republicans added a resolution saying that confiscation was not meant to take a rebel's property beyond his life. When a Confederate planter died, then, his confiscated land would have to be given back to his heirs.

It was a crippling blow. Under such conditions, how could any real land reform be possible? But the freedmen still clung to their belief that they would get land, and keep it. After all, the North was already taking the cotton of the slave owners in conquered territories. Why wouldn't it take the land, too, on which the cotton grew?

Hope rose again when Lincoln allowed some captured plantations to be sold for failure to pay taxes. On the Sea Islands off South Carolina about 17,000 acres of abandoned lands were put up for sale in 1863. Freedmen raised money from their wages, pooled savings, and bought land at public auction.

Then General Grant decided to try an experiment in Mississippi. About twenty-five miles south of Vicksburg, there was a rich piece of land shaped like a pear by the twisting of the river. It was about twelve miles long and twenty-eight miles around. On its nine thousand acres sat six plantations. Because most of the land was owned by Joseph Davis and his brother Jefferson, president of the Confederacy, the peninsula was called Davis Bend. Jefferson, more soldier and politician than planter, had been given a thousand acres by his wealthy brother.

When the Union fleet steamed up the river in 1863, marines went ashore and took over the Davis Bend plantations. The slaves were freed by Grant. He ordered Davis Bend to be set aside as "a suitable place to furnish means and security for the unfortunate race which he [Jefferson Davis] was so instrumental in oppressing. Let the plantations be worked by the freedmen," he said, "and become a Negro paradise."

There was great trouble at first. Confederate guerrillas made raids which killed and wounded many freedmen and drove others off. Then the army worm came and ruined a good part of the crop. But by 1864 about seventy-five ex-slaves were doing well, cultivating their own farms. They had from five to a hundred acres each. Food, mules and equipment were supplied by the army and charged to their accounts. When the crops came in, they marketed them and paid back all their advances. Some had a profit of five hundred to a thousand dollars that year.

The next year, 1865, the blacks took greater control. The army ordered the few white farm operators still on the Bend to leave. The colony was divided into three judicial districts with a sheriff and judge appointed from the blacks. In each district's courts, the jury, counsel, judges, and officers were black. No white man was allowed to interfere in a trial. When an accused freedman was summoned, he had the choice of a trial by jury or by judge alone.

The decisions were reviewed by the Superintendent of Freedmen who sometimes lightened sentences he thought were too severe. The superintendent, John Eaton (who later became U.S. Commissioner of Education) wrote that "the community distinctly demonstrated the capacity of the Negro to take care of himself and exercise under honest and competent direction the functions of self-government."

To take care of orphaned children, the old, and the disabled, the colony set aside five hundred acres of the Jeff Davis plantation for a Home Farm. Whitelaw Reid visited Davis Bend in June 1865, and

stopped at the Jeff Davis plantation. He found the
Confederate leader's home to be much larger than
those of most wealthy planters. Near it stood a
double row of slave quarters. Over the Davis man-
sion was inscribed, "The house that Jeff built."

Now the house was being used as a school.
Two Yankee schoolmarms were teaching the children of the Davis slaves and of runaways from
plantations in the interior. Throughout the colony,
Reid said, about a thousand children were enrolled
in mission schools. The teachers told him the pupils
who could come regularly were making progress
"as rapid as the average progress of white children
in the Northern public schools."

The freedmen showed Reid the jail where the
Davises used to confine their slaves. On Sunday
mornings, the blacks said, "Mass'r Joe" held court
in which he acted as prosecutor, judge, and jury for
the trial of prisoners. Reid found a band of iron,
four inches wide and a half inch thick, with a heavy
chain attached, which the most troublesome slaves
were made to wear while working in the fields. At
night they slept in the jail, with the chain attached
to the wall.

How different this was from the new life at
Davis Bend! Now the freedmen had their own
courts and for the first time knew justice. Visiting

this part of the South about the same time, Thomas Knox found a Plantation Record the slave master had left behind when he fled before the Union troops. On its pages the owner had recorded the daily happenings of his plantation. Some of the entries copied out by Knox reveal what life had been like only a year before:

June 5th: Whipped Harry and Sarah today, because they didn't keep up their rows.

July 7th: Aleck ran away to the woods, because I threatened to whip him.

July 9th: Got Mr. Hall's dogs and hunted Aleck. Didn't find him. Think he is in the swamp back of Brandon's.

July 12: Took Aleck out of Vidalia jail. Paid $4.50 for jail fees. Put him in the stocks when we got home.

July 30th: Moses died this morning. Charles and Henry buried him. His wife was allowed to keep out of the field until noon.

September 9th: John said he was sick this morning, but I made him go to the field. They brought him in before noon. He had a bad fever. Am afraid he won't be able to go out again soon.

September 20th: Whipped Susan, because she didn't pick as much cotton as she did yesterday.

September 29th: Put William in the stocks and

kept him till sunset, for telling Charles he wanted to run away.

December 3rd: Finished picking. Gave the negroes half a holiday.

In a field, Whitelaw Reid watched black militiamen drilling. They were on duty to protect the colony from guerrillas and from the white planters nearby who were bitterly opposed to any changes that lifted the black above his old position. But for the presence of the black troops, the schools and farms scattered around the colony would have been destroyed.

Another 5000 acres of the colony were divided among farmers who formed 181 companies or partnerships. These people—1300 adults and 450 children—managed their own affairs, too, raising crops, selling them, and keeping the profits. Even when the Freedmen's Bureau was established in 1865, its officers were not allowed to meddle with the colony's affairs. The black farmers took care of themselves and showed great initiative in doing it.

The Davis Bend farmers finished 1865 with a profit of $159,200. Fifty of the black planters had made $5000 each. A hundred others had made from $1000 to $4000.

The experiment was a great success, but it was not allowed to go on after 1865. President Johnson pardoned the rebels who had owned the Bend's plantations, and gave them back their land.

A Mississippi historian, Vernon Lane Wharton, had this comment to make about the Davis Bend experiment:

A wiser and more benevolent government might well have seen in Davis Bend the suggestion of a long-time program for making the Negro a self-reliant, prosperous, and enterprising element of the population. It would have cost a great deal of money for the purchase of lands, or would have involved an attack on the sacredness of property rights in their confiscation, but it would certainly have greatly altered the future of the South, and it might have made of her a much happier and more prosperous section.

The same thing happened in the few other places where freedmen had been given a chance to own the land. Some 40,000 blacks had colonized the plantations of the Sea Islands during the war. They, too, made a success of the program. But President Johnson stepped in again. He ordered the lands to be given back to their former rebel owners. The blacks were to leave their farms and go back to work for their old masters.

The freedmen were sick at heart. "They will make freedom a curse to us," one black said, "for we have no home, no land, no oath, no vote, and consequently no country." One abolitionist newspaper asked: "Shall our own, and all coming ages, brand us for the treachery of sacrificing our faithful friends to our and their enemies? God in His mercy save us from such perfidy and such idiocy."

Still, the freedmen did not give up hope. All over the South they heard about the Sea Islands and Davis Bend. Black men had farmed their own land with their own mules. A legend about the coming of "forty acres and a mule" spread everywhere. It was rooted in hope, in need, in justice. They would not give it up, no matter what disappointments came.

In September, 1865, Thaddeus Stevens called for taking away the property of the big Southern landowners. He said the land should be divided up in small parcels, giving forty acres to each adult freedman. Confiscation on that scale was too radical for most Republicans. They shied away from it. But that fall the belief spread through Mississippi that the federal government would give the freedmen land as a Christmas present. The whites heard of it, and knowing Congress had no such intention, feared the disappointed freedmen would rise in

Thaddeus Stevens urging a Congressional committee to divide the property of the big Southern landowners into small parcels, giving forty acres to each freedman.

bloody revolt. Governor Humphreys quickly recruited more militia to force the blacks to give up what arms they had.

Nothing happened that Christmas. Still, the freedmen went on hoping.

Then, in 1866, Congress passed the Southern Homestead Act. It threw open the publicly owned lands of the South that were still unclaimed. Blacks and whites alike could settle on them. In Mississippi there were over three million such acres. Would this be the answer?

It proved a cruel joke. Almost all the land turned out to be useless. It was in the sandy, short-leaf pine region. Nothing worthwhile would grow on it. And even if there had been some usable patches, nothing had been done to provide credit the moneyless freedmen needed for stock and equipment. Eight years later the land was still untouched. No one would buy it even at a nickel an acre.

Some freedmen, giving up all hope of land distribution, tried to buy small tracts in the cotton belt. But the whites refused to sell. Any white landowner who dared to was outlawed by his neighbors. Then the legislature met and wrote into the Black Code the law barring the sale of farm land to any black.

The abolitionists kept pushing for farms for the freedmen. They made speeches, wrote editorials, sent petitions to Congress. Their warnings were prophetic. "Don't you know," they pleaded with Congress, "that if you have 30,000 disloyal nabobs to own more than half the land of the South, they, and nobody else, will *be* the South? *They who own the real estate of a country control its vote.*"

Thomas Wentworth Higginson, colonel of a black regiment in the war, said confiscation "is an essential part of abolition. To give to these people only freedom, without the land, is to give them only the mockery of freedom."

And Wendell Phillips, the great abolitionist spokesman: "What we want to give the Negro is what the masses must have or they are practically serfs, the world over. Land is the usual basis of government," he said. "It is manifestly suicidal, therefore, to leave it in the hands of the hostile party."

Early in 1866, Thad Stevens set before Congress the example of the Czar of Russia who had recently freed 22 million serfs. But the Russian ruler had not cruelly turned the serfs off the land, empty-handed. He had forced their masters to give them homesteads—at a nominal, not the full price—upon the very soil they had farmed, saying, "They have earned this, they have worked upon the land for ages and they are entitled to it."

It did no good. The model of the autocratic czar had no effect upon the democratic legislators. Congress, the President, and the army all failed to develop a sound land policy for the blacks. Historian Henry Steele Commager has pointed out that "At a time when Congress set aside millions of acres for homesteaders in the West and gave over a hundred million acres to railroad corporations, it could not summon up either generosity or vision enough to give land to the freedmen."

By the end of 1867, any chance there might have been to put through land reform had faded. The war was more than two years over, the radical mood had passed, confiscation was a dead issue.

What could the freedmen do? Some managed to achieve independence without any help from government. In Yazoo County, by the fall of 1874, there were 300 blacks who owned real estate. Their holdings ranged from a small house and lot in town to plantations of more than 2000 acres. Many owned horses, mules, sheep, hogs, cows, and chickens. The total property of blacks in the county was appraised at $1,500,000.

For the brief time they knew security under a Reconstruction government, many blacks could and did rise. In Yazoo, said Albert Morgan, whites unused to such competition began to feel there was a danger that "our nigros" would soon "own the whole county." Such minds preached the need for the white race to arm itself so that it could check by force the "threatened supremacy" of the blacks. Soon the policy of terror would succeed in destroying the freedman's hope of a new and better life.

All doors to economic independence had been

As free workers, the blacks get their first pay for working the land.

slammed shut. The freedmen could only go on living on the land, the land that still remained in the hands of ex-slaveholders. They continued to grow cotton for the landlords. Now it was under a variety of local systems that grew up after the war.

Under one arrangement, the freedman rented the land he worked, paying either a fixed sum of money, or a number of bales of cotton, or a share of the crop. In another, he worked a piece of land under the planter's direction and got part of the crop in return. Sharecropping, they called this. In the last system, he worked on the farm as a laborer, paid in cash by the day, week, or month.

Most freedmen, then, became sharecroppers, renters, or wage hands. If they couldn't own the land, they often preferred to rent. This gave them more freedom and the chance to make some profit. But the Mississippi whites were against this, too, and the law that barred the purchase of land also barred renting it. In Hinds County, the whites pledged not to rent to freedmen, and denounced anyone who didn't follow their rule as "an enemy to the interests of the country."

Sharecropping became by far the most common system in Mississippi, as in most of the South.

It wasn't slave labor—not legally—but to the freedmen on the plantations, life didn't feel much different from slavery. The planters still owned all the land. They still pocketed all the money. They still made all the rules.

6

A revolution begins

As early as 1863, Frederick Douglass told the country boldly that he would demand for the emancipated slaves nothing less than "the most perfect civil and political equality. The right to vote," he said, "is the only solid and final solution of the problem before us."

But of all the proposals made for Reconstruction, this was the one the country had the hardest time accepting. Not even the abolitionists could agree on the matter of giving the freedmen the unrestricted right to vote. Some opposed it on the ground the freedmen were illiterate and ignorant. To this Carl Schurz replied: "Practical liberty is a good school. . . . It is idle to say that it will be time to speak of Negro suffrage when the whole colored race will be educated, for the ballot may be necessary to him to secure his education."

Some who approved black suffrage did so asking such qualifications as ability to read and write, payment of taxes, or establishment in a trade.

Only five states in the North, it was pointed out, let blacks vote. And none of these had large Negro populations. Public opinion was plainly against black suffrage. Between 1865 and 1868, eight northern and midwestern states refused blacks the right to vote. Even Thaddeus Stevens hesitated to press for the freedman's vote while the majority of his party were so openly opposed.

But powerful political and economic considerations brought about a change in 1867. The North was angered by the refusal of most Southern states to ratify the Fourteenth Amendment protecting Negro citizenship, by the adoption of the Black Codes, and by the growing violence against the freedmen. In the middle of 1866, anti-Negro riots in Memphis and New Orleans caused the death of eighty blacks. Idealists argued that the freedmen needed the ballot to defend their freedom, to protect their civil rights, their welfare, their livelihoods.

Now it was time to move, Stevens saw. The Republican Party was beginning to understand that if the Confederate states came back in without the blacks being given the vote, Democrats—not Republicans—would fill all those seats in Congress. And no politician wanted to see his party outvoted.

Nor did Northern businessmen want to see Congress dominated by Democrats. On most of the economic issues of the day—taxation, the national debt, railroads, regulation of corporations, government aid to business, protective tariff—the Southern Democrats were opposed to Northern business. So this powerful force, too, was ready to go the whole way with Thad Stevens.

In March, 1867, Congress took over the full job of Reconstruction. It divided the South into five military districts controlled by martial law. It took the vote away from large numbers of rebel whites. It declared all black men could vote and hold office. And it ordered elections for conventions to write new constitutions for the rebel states.

The ex-Confederates were stunned. Mississippi Governor Humphreys tried to get the Supreme Court to halt Reconstruction, but it refused to interfere.

The political revolution had begun in the South.

The first stage—in Mississippi as everywhere—was to register the new electorate.

The Southern Democrats debated what to do. Some wanted to register and vote against the constitutional convention. Mississippi's leaders, seeing which way the wind was blowing, decided to sail with it. Better to stop fighting, and live with the reality, they reasoned. They had no desire to live under military rule. The sooner the state got back into the Union, the better. If they didn't make some show of cooperating with Congress, more radical measures might be taken against them. The specter of sweeping land confiscation still haunted them.

Just as important, they thought, was the need to move fast to gain control of the new voters before the Radical Republicans could organize them. Letters began to appear in the papers telling the freedmen, "Trust us: your white friends are eager to help you make a good start in the new South." In a speech to a mixed audience of blacks and whites, one of the old fire-eaters, Albert G. Brown, said: "I am not only willing, but anxious, to instruct the Negro in the ABC's of his politics."

But it didn't work. Few freedmen paid any

attention to these speeches about "mutual interests" and "cooperation" and "friendship" and "harmony." Who could believe such talk? The tune was different, but the voice was still old master's. And in hundreds of instances over the past two years, the whites had made all too clear their real belief that blacks deserved only what crumbs might drop from the master's table.

Many whites now decided to sit down and wait it out. They just couldn't believe something new was happening. But blacks rushed headlong into political life. They joined the Republican Party, held meetings, made speeches, marched in parades. On the appointed day, they came into the registration offices by the hundreds, quiet, orderly, but many carrying arms.

Much of the electoral work among the freedmen was done by the Union Leagues. These societies had been organized in the North during the war by the Republican Party. They worked for emancipation and the defeat of the Confederacy. Now the Leagues had come South to marshal votes for the Republican Party. They showed the freedmen how to register and explained the rights and duties of voting.

Alarmed by the extremely rapid spread of the

League clubs, the whites tried to discourage blacks from political action. The Vicksburg *Times* suggested ways of putting on the pressure:

Others may do as they please, but if men will protect and shelter vipers, they must take the consequences. We shall prepare and publish a list of merchants who keep negro radicals as porters and laborers, and advise our people to avoid all such shops. Hotels who employ negro waiters and porters who belong to Loyal Leagues, will also be published, and the public warned against them. Draymen, hackmen, barbers, and all other negro laborers who belong to the Loyal Leagues, shall in like manner be published. . . . The Southern Democrat who feeds a radical, black or white, is false to his race, false to his country, false to God and false to himself. He who supports them in any shape is a COWARD who disgraces the name of man.

What political choice did the freedmen have? On one side were the native whites who had held them in slavery, resisted emancipation, adopted the Black Code. On the other were the Radical Republicans, men who had pressed hard for emancipation, had urged the arming of blacks, had insisted on civil and political equality.

Naturally, black voters believed it was to their

best interests to join and work for the Republican Party. It was the only party that promised to support their ideals.

When registration ended in Mississippi, the results astonished the ex-rebels. The freedmen were in a big majority: 60,000 as against 47,000. Of the sixty-one counties, thirty-three showed black majorities. That settled any doubts Southern whites may have had about whether freedmen were interested in politics.

In five of the eleven Confederate states, blacks registered a majority. Altogether in the South, more than 703,000 blacks and 627,000 whites became qualified voters.

With registration completed, General Ord now set an election for November. It would determine whether the voters wanted a constitutional convention as a step toward getting the state back into the Union, or whether they preferred to stay under military rule and be without representation in Congress. Delegates to the convention would be elected at the same time.

Disgusted by the prospect of what they called "African rule," many whites decided not to take part in the election. They called it a "shameful humiliation" when General Ord chose blacks as judges and clerks of the election, and appointed an ex-slave,

B. T. Montgomery, the justice of peace at Davis
Bend. Montgomery, the first black to hold a state
office, had managed the plantations of Jefferson
Davis and his brother Joe before the war.

The Reconstructionists won the November election by a big majority: 70,000 voted for a convention and only 6000 against. And the Republicans
took most of the delegates.

In January, the delegates met in Jackson to
write a new constitution for Mississippi.

It was the strangest political gathering the state
had ever seen. For the first time in Mississippi's
history, black Americans were represented. Sixteen
black Republicans sat amid the one hundred delegates. Among the other eighty-four delegates were
fifty-five more Republicans, and twenty-nine conservatives, all white.

None of the blacks had ever held public office
before. Only a few years earlier they and all their
people had had no rights a white man was bound to
respect. Now they had registered, voted, been
elected to office, and were about to help draft the
basic law of their state.

It should be noted that although blacks were
a majority of both the population and of the registered voters, they numbered only sixteen percent of
the delegates. They had made no attempt to "take

The liberated blacks meet in convention to discuss the problems of Reconstruction. Their deliberations helped shape the most progressive state constitution the South had ever known.

over" the convention. But the fact that any black men at all were sitting down to make the law seemed unbelievable to white conservatives. Filled with horror and disgust, they could see the blacks only as "ragamuffins," "jailbirds," "baboons," "monkeys," or "mules."

For 115 days the delegates worked on the new constitution. In the end they created a document that sealed the death of slavery and opened a path to the first true democracy Mississippi would live under.

The new constitution provided for black suffrage. It banned property qualifications for voting. It barred from office any who had fought for or aided the Confederacy. It assured equality on all public means of transport.

Property rights of women were recognized. Jailing for debt was forbidden. A public school system was provided for all children from five to twenty-one. The courts were modernized. Local government was made more democratic.

The constitution was hardly written when a fight began over its adoption. It was to be submitted to the voters for approval in June. At the same time, they would elect state officers, the legislature, and members of Congress.

Governer Humphreys so bitterly opposed the constitution that the military commander removed him from office. In his place, a thirty-three-year-old soldier from an abolitionist family in Maine, General Adelbert Ames, was appointed acting governor. Ames was a tall, handsome man who had graduated from West Point and earned the Medal of Honor on the battlefield of Bull Run. He soon demonstrated his skill as an administrator of state

affairs and his sympathy for the cause of the freedmen. Years later he wrote that when Reconstruction
began he felt he "had a mission with a large M. . . .
I believe that I could render [the freedmen] a great
service. I felt that I had a mission to perform in
their interest, and I unhesitatingly consented to
represent them, and unite my fortunes with them."

The Democrats swiftly organized to defeat the
new constitution. They campaigned hardest in the
plantation districts where most of the blacks lived.
They threatened to fire the freedmen and white
farmers from their jobs or evict them from their
farms if they voted for the constitution. Vote our
way, or it's "eternal war," they said.

The Republicans, possibly trying to play it
safe, did not nominate a single black for state or
county office. Still weakly organized in the state,
the party could not get out the maximum vote or
put forth trained black leaders.

As a result, the constitution was defeated. It
meant the military would continue to rule the state.
The Democrats were delighted. They thought they
had only to wait for the national elections in November, when the Radicals would be driven out of
Congress. In July, the Fourteenth Amendment to
the Constitution was adopted, giving blacks citizenship and promising them equal protection of the

laws. And in November the Republicans won a great victory in the national elections. They took over Congress and put General Grant in the White House. The day after Grant was inaugurated, he asked Acting Governor Ames to be military commander of Mississippi as well. Holding both jobs, Ames now had great power over all affairs in the state. He immediately removed many of the local officials who were blocking Reconstruction policy. In their place he appointed many blacks.

A new election was slated for the fall of 1869. The voters would again decide on the constitution and elect state officers.

The Democrats tried a new tack. They decided it was better to get the state back into the Union and pick up their fight for white supremacy afterward. They melted their party into a new one, calling it the National Union Republican Party, picked President Grant's brother-in-law, Lewis A. Dent, for governor. Dent owned a Delta plantation but lived in Washington, in the White House. The fact that he was a thousand miles from Mississippi didn't bother the new party's leaders. They even nominated a black, Thomas Sinclair, for secretary of state. These were clever moves aimed at splitting the white Republican vote of Grant's followers and the black vote.

The Radical Republicans nominated James L. Alcorn for governor. He was typical of many rich whites in the state who decided to join the Republicans. Although one of Mississippi's biggest planters and slaveholders, with 12,000 acres in Coahoma County, he had opposed secession. Nevertheless, he went along with his state and fought briefly in the Confederate Army. When defeat came, he was one of the first Southerners to admit secession had been a mistake. He even called it treasonable.

Alcorn was willing to work with the freedmen, in the hope of winning their support for his own class's program. As a planter, he wanted the state to rebuild the levees and the railroads and to cut taxes on land. In return, he supported civil rights measures, a school program, and a better court system. He was being a realist. If he couldn't have everything he wanted, he would take what he could get. Meanwhile as governor, he thought, he would be in a good position to keep equality from going too far.

For secretary of state the Radical Republicans also named a black man. He was the Reverend James D. Lynch. An educated Pennsylvanian, he helped start the schools in Savannah under General Sherman. Then he had come to Mississippi to head the Methodist Episcopal Church in Jackson—almost entirely black. He worked too as an agent of the Freedmen's Bureau. He had superb talents and earned wide popularity, even among the whites. A leading Democrat, W. H. Hardy, had this to say of him:

He was a great orator; fluent and graceful, he stirred his great audiences as no other man did or could do. He was the idol of Negroes, who would come from every point of the compass for miles, on foot, to hear him speak. He rarely spoke to less than a thousand, and often two to five thousand. . . . Imagine one or two thousand Negroes standing en masse in a semi-circle facing the speaker, whose tones were as clear and resonant as a silver bell, and of a sudden, every throat would be wide open, and a spontaneous shout in perfect unison would arise, and swell, and subside as the voice of one man . . .

The situation looked confusing. Here were the Democrats supporting a slate topped by a Northerner and a black man, and the Republicans supporting a former slaveholder. But the black Mississippians saw to the heart of the matter. Sinclair didn't fool them. He was "Uncle Thomas" Sinclair. They knew the Republicans wanted to improve the position of the freedman, while the Democrats wanted to hold him back.

In November, the new constitution won the voters' approval. And Alcorn and his party gained the state offices by a big majority.

Mississippi was reconstructed at last—more than four years after the war's end. With blacks voting and blacks holding office, it came back into the Union.

7

A government of the people, by the people, for the people

On January 11, 1870, Mississippi's first Reconstruction legislature met in Jackson. No body of
lawmakers such as this had ever before assembled
in the state. Their color was different. And so was
their politics.

There were thirty-five blacks in that newborn
legislature, thirty-five out of 140 members. Thirty
of the blacks sat in the lower House, five in the
Senate. There were sixty-six Republicans to forty-
nine Democrats, giving the Republicans a comfort-
able majority.

Ten years earlier, if anyone had suggested black men might one day be full citizens of Mississippi, voting and holding office, he would have been thought crazy. In no state of the Old South would anyone have taken such an idea seriously. But especially in Mississippi. For this state, so remote, still very much the lawless frontier, its huge plantations ruled like absolute monarchies, had known nothing of democracy.

On this day, some of these same wealthy plantation counties were represented in the legislature by men who had recently been slaves.

Warren County, where Vicksburg is, had sent four blacks to the legislature. Hinds County, where Jackson, the state capital, is located, sent two black representatives and one black senator. Adams, holding Natchez, sent three blacks to the House and one to the Senate. Washington, whose chief town is Greenville, sent two black representatives and one black senator. Holmes, Panola, Wilkinson, and Noxubee Counties all sent one or more blacks.

The names and counties deserve to be remembered in Mississippi's history:

IN THE HOUSE OF REPRESENTATIVES:
> Adams: John R. Lynch, H. P. Jacobs
> Bolivar: C. M. Bowles
> Chickasaw: Ambrose Henderson

Claiborne: M. T. Newsom
Copiah: Emanuel Handy
Hinds: Henry Mayson, C. F. Norris
Holmes: Edmund Scarborough, Cicero
    Mitchell
Issaquena: Richard Griggs
Jefferson: Merrimon Howard
Lauderdale: J. Aaron Moore
Lawrence: George Charles
Lowndes: J. F. Bolden
Madison: Dr. J. J. Spellman
Monroe: William Holmes
Noxubee: Isham Stewart, Nathan McNeese,
    A. K. Davis
Oktibeeha: David Higgins
Panola: C. A. Yancey, J. H. Piles
Warren: Charles P. Head, Peter Borrow,
    Albert Johnson
Washington: John Morgan, Dr. Stites
Wilkinson: H. M. Foley, George W. White
Yazoo: W. H. Foote

IN THE SENATE:

Adams: Rev. Hiram R. Revels
Hinds: Charles Caldwell
Lowndes: Robert Gleed
Warren: Rev. T. W. Stringer
Washington: Rev. William Gray

Besides these men, many of them ex-slaves, there were white Republicans from the North who had recently settled in the state, many of them ex-Union soldiers. Together with some native white Republicans, they added up to a large majority who could outvote the old white class that once held all the political power.

Most of the history books have damned the two classes of white men, labeling them "carpetbaggers" and "scalawags." They picture the first as greedy Yankees who came south with so little property they could carry it all in a carpetbag. Supposedly they saw in the new Reconstruction governments a chance to grab power and get rich quick. The legend holds they were all villains who took advantage of the new black voters.

But recent studies show most of the carpetbaggers were young Union army veterans who sought land and opportunity in the South *before* passage of the Reconstruction Acts of 1867. They were teachers and preachers, merchants and mechanics, businessmen and industrialists who saw a new economic frontier in the underdeveloped South. (The same restlessness or desire to get ahead drove other men to go west or north at other times.) The vast majority in Mississippi were men who had come as planters. They bought or leased planta-

The freedmen moved rapidly into political life. Here, a black U.S. deputy marshal and a black policeman help watch the polls during an election.

---

tions, they hired freedmen, they paid cash for everything. They pumped badly needed money into the South's economy.

Contrary to the legend, most of the newcomers lost their investment. Inexperience, bad weather,

crop failures, boycotts by Southerners who refused
to deal with the Northerners—these and other fac-
tors caused a great many Yankees to give up in a
year or two and return to the North.

Those who stayed were the ones who entered
state and local politics in 1867 or later. Of course,
the native whites detested these northern Republicans, especially when they joined with the freedmen in political action.

One of Mississippi's best-known carpetbaggers
was young Albert T. Morgan. Hated by the whites,
he was elected to office again and again by the
blacks. Born in New York, he came from a Baptist
family which moved to a Wisconsin farm. The
Morgan children were bred to hate slavery and believe in racial equality. At eighteen, Albert left
Oberlin College when Sumter fell, and enlisted in
the Union Army. He fought from Bull Run to Lee's
surrender, attaining the rank of lieutenant colonel
despite his youth. A few months after the war
ended, Albert and his older brother Charles, also
a veteran Union officer, came to Mississippi and
leased a plantation in Yazoo County. They were
not concerned with politics at first, but wanted only
to prosper and build permanent homes in this rich
river valley they had come to love. They expected

a tide of emigrants moving southward would in twenty-five years lay the foundations of a new empire in the Mississippi lowlands by building canals, railroads, schools, farms, and factories.

When they came, the Morgan brothers brought enough capital to lease a 900-acre plantation for three years and built a sawmill which trained workers from the North operated. The Morgans offered good wages and working conditions to a plantation force of 125 freedmen, who much preferred working for the Yankees than for their old masters. For two years the Morgans labored, and success seemed assured, when "white" justice in Yazoo cheated them out of their property. By 1867 they had lost $50,000 and all their holdings. Nineteen other ex-federal officers and soldiers in their county—engaged in planting, merchandising, or manufacturing—fell victim to the same outrages. The "we-all Southerners," as Morgan put it, succeeded in ruining "them damned Yankees."

About this time, Congress voted the Radical Reconstruction program, and Morgan was asked by his black neighbors to run for office. He was elected delegate to the constitutional convention, and then state senator on the Alcorn ticket. In 1873, he became the county sheriff. By now he was a marked

man, hounded, insulted, attacked at every opportunity by white Democrats who hated him even
more than they hated most Northerners. The rea-
son? In 1870 Colonel Morgan had married a beauti-
ful young black teacher, Carolyn Highgate. Born
in Syracuse, New York, she had come to Jackson to
teach in a school set up by the Freedmen's Bureau.
Morgan had fallen in love with her at first sight,
and he married her as soon as the Mississippi legislature passed a bill he introduced, overthrowing the
old anti-miscegenation law and permitting inter-
racial marriages. He and Carrie set up housekeep-
ing in Yazoo City, an act that made the racists all
the more determined to kill or drive out this carpetbagger.

The scalawags were lumped together as ignorant poor whites taken in by the carpetbaggers.
They were denounced as renegade Southerners who
sold themselves for office. But these native Southern whites were of many kinds. Some were former
Confederates who thought it best to throw in their
lot with the winners. Others, like the wealthy James
Alcorn, had opposed secession in 1860 and now
favored the Republican plans for building up the
South. He was ready to grant the blacks legal
equality in the hope of gaining their political support for measures that would encourage economic

growth. Many scalawags were poor whites who hated the old planter class and hoped the radical program would give them a bigger stake in life.

The Republicans organized the leadership and committees of the legislature, shaped the bills, and set the public policy of the new Mississippi.

At once the legislature ratified the Fourteenth and Fifteenth Amendments to the U.S. Constitution. (The Fifteenth, recently adopted by Congress, gave blacks the right to vote.) That completed the state's reconstruction. Now it was accepted back into the Union. Military rule of Mississippi ended and civil government took over.

An immediate task for the legislature was to elect men to the two long-term vacancies in the U.S. Senate, and to pick someone to fill the uncompleted Senate term of Jefferson Davis. General Ames and Governor Alcorn were chosen for the full-term seats and the Republican caucus settled on Hiram Revels, a black minister from Natchez, for the short-term seat.

Then the legislature wiped the old injustices off the slate. Its goal, it declared, was to get rid of all laws "which in any manner recognized any natural difference or distinction between citizens and inhabitants of the state, or which in any manner or in any degree, discriminate between citizens or inhabitants of this State, founded on race, color, or previous condition of servitude."

The lawmakers, therefore, repealed at once the old slave code and the Black Code of 1865, as well as all other discriminatory laws regarding jury service, travel on railroads, steamboats or stagecoaches, or seating in theaters.

These were great things to do. It was much harder to take a state which had been ruined by a long war and put it back into operation. Only this time, to do it with justice for all and concern for the welfare of every man, black or white.

To carry out such a program costs money. Mississippi had almost no credit. The state treasury held fifty dollars. Agriculture and business had to be encouraged. Property had to be taxed to pay the expenses of government.

A prime task was to start a public school system. The state had almost no schools. It would take vast sums of money to build an educational system, staff it, and operate it.

The courts were out-of-date in form and methods. The old judges were tied to the old order. Drastic reforms were needed, as well as new men to sit on the bench. One difficulty was to find men with legal training and with concern for building and protecting the new democracy and *all* its citizens' rights.

The legislature struggled daily with these tough problems. Men who had not been allowed to learn to read and write now shared in the job of planning a whole new educational system for themselves and their children. Men who had only a pair of overalls to their names were figuring out how to raise millions to finance a state's needs.

Month after month they studied, argued, debated, drafted bills, rewrote them, sought common interests, learned to strike compromises. Out of their work came an educational system far beyond anything the state had ever known. They reorganized the court system, and gave it a new code of laws. They modernized old public buildings and built new ones. They set up state hospitals in Natchez and Vicksburg. · They opened new facilities for the blind, the deaf, the dumb, the insane.

To protect the workingman's interests, they abolished all vagrancy laws, and lowered the tax rates on the tools and implements of mechanics and artisans. The rights of women were protected by laws that made employers pay married women's wages to them, instead of to their husbands, and that prevented a husband from selling a homestead without his wife's consent.

To encourage the expansion of business and industry, the lawmakers granted charters to a great many railroads, banks, public utilities, mining, and manufacturing companies.

The money needed for the great program of reconstruction had to come from taxation. All the progressive changes made by the new government raised the state's expenses. The old regime had done none of these things. When the planters ruled the state, they laughed at free education for "niggers" and "poor white trash." Their sole aim was to run things to suit their own narrow interests and to keep the cost of it to themselves way down. Before the war, land and slaves were placed at low valuation, which meant low taxes on planters. The merchants, bankers, and professionals were the ones made to pay stiff taxes, many times higher than for the planters.

All that was changed now. Taxes were placed on a uniform basis so that all property was taxed at its full value. If the social needs of the people increased, the government raised the tax rate to meet the needs.

The planters naturally made a big outcry against the new taxation. They accused the legislature of "fearful" and "monstrous" corruption, of unnecessary expenses, of trying to raise taxes to the point of confiscation. But the truth was, taxation really amounted to less than nine mills on the dollar, not at all a "monstrous" rate.

In six months, the legislature passed 325 acts and resolutions. People were pleased, and in 1872, the Republicans again won a sweeping victory.

8

Reading
and writing

"There is no doubt," wrote W. E. B. DuBois, "but that the thirst of the black man for knowledge . . . gave birth to the public free-school of the South. It was the question upon which black voters and legislators insisted more than anything else."

Before the war, Mississippi had paid lip service to the value of public education. She had done little about it. Funds granted the state for this purpose by the federal government had been badly mismanaged and lost. Generations of black and white children grew up in ignorance.

At the time of emancipation, illiteracy among the Southern blacks was over 95 percent. Less than 150,000 of the four million freedmen could read and write. For whites, too, there was no public education system, except in North Carolina.

When the Union Army opened up Mississippi country, the missionary societies began to offer education to the blacks. But some freedmen had not waited for outside help. In Natchez, black women had opened up three schools on their own. One of these teachers was reported to have run a secret night school for Natchez slaves before the war. When James E. Yeatman, a northern agent, headed into the back country to see what was going on, he was astonished at what he found in just one neighborhood:

There is at Groshon's plantation a school taught by Rose Anna, a colored girl. She has between 50 and 100 scholars. Uncle Jack, a colored man, at the Goodrich place, is teaching a school of 81 scholars. Uncle Tom, a colored man at the Savage plantation, has a school of 30 scholars. He is infirm, and teaches them remaining himself in bed. Wm. McCutchen, a colored man, has commenced a school on the Currie place. He

A freedmen's school in Vicksburg, where children of all ages were taught by one of the many brave women who came from the North.

---

has 63 scholars. . . . He has but one arm, having lost the other by a cotton gin.

Where the freedmen had come into Union lines, the work of educating them began at once. It was hard to find suitable buildings and equipment.

Churches and confiscated mansions were used, barns, tents, old barracks, empty hotels. Often schools met in tumbledown sheds or cabins, with two or three classes reciting at once in the same room.

One teacher reported that she "opened school here in a rough log house, thirty feet square and so open that the crevices admitted light sufficient without the aid of windows. The furniture consisted of undressed plank benches, without backs, from ten to twelve feet long, and in the center of the room stood an old steamboat stove about four feet long which had been taken out of the river."

Another teacher wrote her school was in a shed that had no floor. In bad weather the rain swept through the places where the windows should have been. "I have to huddle the children first in one corner and then in another to keep them from drowning or swamping."

Few teachers began with the books, charts, or slates they needed. Sometimes it took weeks or months after school opened before the supplies arrived.

The schools were crowded with eager pupils of all ages. Without enough desks or benches, the pupils often sat against the walls or in the aisles on the floor. But discomfort kept no one away. To the

In many schools, mothers and fathers sat with their children to learn the ABC's.

---

black students, schools and reading and writing were the symbols of freedom. Education was their guarantee against the return of slavery. After his travels south, Whitelaw Reid concluded the freedmen "were far more eager than any other to secure the advantages of education for themselves, and especially for their children."

The first teachers who came to help in Mississippi were sent by the American Missionary Association, the Western Freedmen's Aid Commission, the National Freedmen's Relief Association, and the Society of Friends—the Quakers. Later they were joined by other church groups. Soon there were ten thousand such teachers spread through the South. Each society set up its own schools and ran them as it wished, until, in the fall of 1864, the Superintendent of Freedmen took over control of the schools. Fees from twenty-five cents to $1.50 per month were charged the pupils to make the schools self-supporting. Those who couldn't pay came free. The program grew rapidly. By January 1866, there were sixty-eight schools in the state with over 5000 pupils. Throughout the South, there were over 90,000 black pupils, studying in 740 schools. But still, the schools were reaching only a small part of the black population.

Southern whites had never believed in education for blacks. Now that it had come, they bitterly fought it. In Yazoo City, when the Freedmen's Bureau supplied the lumber to build a school for the blacks, the local white mechanics refused to erect it "for love or money." They threatened to kill "any damned Yankee" who would "dare to strike a lick" on such a job. But half a dozen white workers from the Morgan sawmill took over the job under the protection of a squad of federal troops. Some

Southerners spoke with contempt of the "nigger teachers" and called them the "scum" from the North. Women of abolitionist convictions and with deep religious faith were labelled "prostitutes." The fact that so many of the teachers were white women made their enemies all the angrier.

Prejudice moved beyond insults and refusal to accept the teachers socially. The teachers, whose pay came in irregularly, were often denied credit at the stores. Most white homes were barred to them when they looked for places to live. A number of teachers stayed with the freedmen's families.

The most vicious opponents of education turned to violence. Black pupils were stoned in the streets or school yards, rocks were thrown through the school windows while classes were in session, the buildings were broken into at night and robbed or wrecked. Some were burned down. Teachers were publicly whipped and ordered to leave town at peril of their lives.

This persecution added to the troubles of an educational system always suffering from a shortage of teachers. The North responded generously to the cry for help. Many brave women, white and black, came South to teach the freedmen. But the number was not enough to meet the needs of four million ex-slaves. In 1870, only one-tenth of the black children of school age were actually in school.

Though Southern blacks had been denied the right to learn, there were a number who had managed to educate themselves in slavery times. To add to them, many white teachers enlisted their older and more advanced black students, using them as assistant teachers. What these apprentices learned one day they taught the younger children the next.

The students were of all sizes and ages. Sometimes three generations of one family came to class hand-in-hand. Child or adult, all were eager students from the day the school doors opened. The adults often came to class in the late afternoon or evening, after the day's work was done. Some took the spellers and readers to the field with them, to study while resting.

The basic lessons were in reading, writing, spelling, and arithmetic. History and geography were taught to advanced classes. Religion was usually part of the program because most of the teachers were sent in by missionary groups.

The first postwar government in Mississippi, all-white, had done nothing for education. A Vicksburg paper spoke its views: "If any radical was ever black enough to suppose the people of Mississippi would endow negro schools . . . such chaps had better take to marching on with John Brown's soul; they will hardly reach the object of their desires short of the locality where John is kicking and waiting. The State has not opened them, nor has she the slightest idea of doing anything of the kind."

When Mississippi's Reconstruction government took office, it established schooling for *all* children between the ages of five and twenty-one years. A poll tax was levied to pay the cost. Local school boards were set up which had to open schools wherever the parents of twenty-five children asked for them. Classes had to be operated for at least four months of the year.

In the first year of free education, the state opened 3000 schools, attended by 66,000 pupils. Mississippi hired 3500 teachers, paying them an average salary of $60 a month. The ex-slaveholders hated the expense of educating their former slaves. The native white women refused to teach black children, so the job continued to be done chiefly by Northern men and women.

Opposition to the black schools never let up during Reconstruction. In Monroe County the Ku Klux Klan, a secret society formed to terrorize the freedmen, forced twenty-six teachers to close their schools. In Lowndes County several teachers were whipped and many schools broken up by the KKK. In Noxubee County three of four schoolhouses were burned down. In Winston, every build-

Members of the Ku Klux Klan, with guns, hooded masks, and robes. Opposed to education for blacks, they tried to destroy the schools.

ing in the county where school was being taught, except one, was burned.

The Klan, formed in Tennessee right after the war, soon appeared in Mississippi. Confederate General Nathan Bedford Forrest, wealthy planter and slave trader, was its first Grand Wizard, and some of the most prominent citizens were among its leaders. The Klan organized local gangs of thugs who dressed in white robes and hoods and rode white-sheeted horses. They wanted to frighten poor whites and blacks and stop them from working together to solve their common problems. The Klansmen roved the countryside at night, whipping and murdering black and white Republican leaders. They burned churches as well as schools and soon began killing black preachers and farmers and Jewish merchants. They tortured or lynched blacks for any excuse. Men, women, and children fell victim to their brutality. A state law to stop the Klan was passed in 1870, but officers refused to make arrests, witnesses feared to testify, and judges punished with light fines that never were collected. Federal laws against the KKK, backed by arrest, heavy fines, and jail sentences finally broke its power. By 1872, the Klan had faded, but other bands of terrorists took its place.

For the two years between March, 1869, and

March, 1871, the Mississippi records show at least
two hundred people died, victims of the terror.

Many years later, the ex-slave Pierce Harper,
recalled what the Klan had done in his neighborhood:

After us colored folks was 'sidered free and turned loose,
the Ku Klux broke out. Some colored people started to
farming, like I told you, and gathered the old stock. If
they got so they made good money and had a good
farm, the Ku Klux would come and murder 'em. The
government builded schoolhouses, and the Ku Klux
went to work and burned 'em down. They'd go to the
jails and take the colored men out and knock their
brains out and break their necks and throw 'em in the
river.

There was a colored man they taken, his name was
Jim Freeman. They taken him and destroyed his stuff
and him 'cause he was making some money. Hung him
in a tree in his front yard, right in front of his cabin.

There was some colored young men went to the
schools they'd opened by the government. Some white
woman said someone had stole something of hers, so
they put them young men in jail. The Ku Klux went
to jail and took 'em out and killed 'em. That happened
the second year after the war.

After the Ku Kluxers got so strong, the colored

The KKK posted these warnings to frighten the freedmen. Reconstruction leaders were whipped and killed by the Klan.

men got together and made the complaint before the
law. The governor told the law to give 'em the guns
in the commissary, what the Southern soldiers had
used, so they issued the colored men old muskets and
said protect themselves. They got together and organized the militia and had leaders like regular soldiers.
They didn't meet 'cept when they heard the Ku
Kluxers was coming to get some colored folks. They
was ready for 'em. They'd hide in the cabins, and
then's when they found out who a lot of them Ku
Kluxes was, 'cause a lot of 'em was kilt. They wore long
sheets and covered the hosses with sheets so you
couldn't recognize 'em. Men you thought was your
friend was Ku Kluxes, and you'd deal with 'em in
stores in the daytime, and at night they'd come out to
your house and kill you.

In the beginning, Mississippi whites believed
the Reconstruction government would have both
blacks and whites attending the same schools. The
convention writing the new constitution had first
defeated a proposal requiring segregation. Then
it voted down a proposal barring segregation. As a
result, the constitution said nothing at all about the
issue. There was no policy one way or the other.

Black leaders agreed that nonsegregated education was the ideal. But they differed on how and when that goal was to be realized. The whites were solidly against it, and threatened a race war if the schools were "mixed." Some black spokesmen demanded the issue be met squarely, and right now. But the majority seemed to think that under mass education, in a separated school system, the whites would be educated out of their prejudices. And then the schools could be organized without regard to race. They pointed out, too, that separate schools were desired not only by the whites. For the time being, many black parents thought it would be better for their children to go to separate schools while race prejudice was still so strong. The main thing, they felt, was not the question of segregation, but a way to open up educational opportunity for their people wherever they could.

The various missionary groups had operated separate schools in the South all along. Separation in education became the rule all through Reconstruction, not only in Mississippi, but everywhere in the South.

Nevertheless, the blacks were determined to get equal school facilities. In Yazoo County, for instance, where there were 2180 whites of school age and 4183 blacks in 1872, the school board had established only twenty-five schools for the blacks

Schools put up for the freedmen were burned down by whites.

and given forty-one to the white children. The freedmen fought against this inequity, and by 1875, there were forty-five for whites and sixty-three for blacks.

To help advance higher education for blacks, the Reconstruction legislature opened two teacher training colleges at Holly Springs and Tougaloo, and established Alcorn University (now in Lorman) as a counterpart to the state university. Fellowships were provided and money for expenses in addition to free tuition.

The gains made in education during Reconstruction were impressive. "It was an amazing advance beyond anything the state had known before," wrote historian Vernon Lane Wharton. That it fell far short of the need was not the fault of the freedmen. Still, thousands—black and white—made the tremendous leap from darkness to light, from ignorance to knowledge.

9

Black power

Black power in government was the high point of Reconstruction. It was the first time blacks shared in the political life of their towns, counties, state, and federal government. But never did they "rule" the South. At no time in Reconstruction did blacks control a state.

Although blacks were in the majority of the population in the states of Mississippi, Louisiana, and South Carolina, they did not dominate those governments. In South Carolina, they showed their

greatest strength. Twice they elected black lieutenant governors and speakers of the house. One
black became state treasurer, another secretary of
state, and a third sat on the state supreme court.
But whites always held the governor's post, and
usually controlled the two branches of the legislature.

In Mississippi, blacks held about a third of the
seats of the first Reconstruction legislature. During
the years of Reconstruction they elected a lieutenant governor, a secretary of state, a superintendent of education, a U.S. Congressman, and two
U.S. Senators.

In addition to James D. Lynch, there were
many other blacks who made distinguished records
in Mississippi politics. Another Lynch—unrelated
—was John R. His long career was even more remarkable. Originally from Louisiana, he was born
of a slave mother and a white planter in 1847.
When the father died, sixteen-year-old John and
his mother were sold and taken to Natchez. John,
a very handsome boy, had been tutored in Louisiana. He became the servant of one of Natchez's
leading citizens, and was freed when the Union
troops came in. He was lucky to find a job in a
photographer's studio across the alley from a school
for whites. He used to keep an ear cocked to hear

the lessons in the classroom and with his superior intelligence was able to keep up with the courses taught.

Young Lynch moved into politics when he was made a justice of the peace. At twenty-two, he was elected to the state legislature. Because of his youth, his self-confidence, his skill as a speaker, and his ready wit, he made a powerful impression. Quickly he was made Speaker of the House, and within a year was elected to Congress. He came to Washington in 1873 as the youngest member of the House of Representatives. His talent as a debater made Democrats fear to clash with him. In Congress, he served three terms, earning great respect from both friend and foe. The historian Wharton said that Lynch "probably possessed as much influence at the White House as any Negro has ever had." Presidents Grant and Garfield often called him in for consultation.

After Reconstruction, Lynch served as fourth auditor of the U.S. Treasury under President Harrison. He practiced law for some years, then served in the army for thirteen years, retiring as a major to enter law again. Moving to Chicago, he became a leader in that city's Republican organization. He died in 1939, at the age of ninety-three.

Some of the earliest black political leaders in

Mississippi came to prominence in the constitutional convention. The most important was Charles Caldwell, who had been a slave blacksmith in Clinton, a village close to the state capital. A man of great intelligence, he had managed to educate himself. He showed natural ability as a leader, and rapidly earned strong influence in the Republican Party. Caldwell's fearlessness became legendary in 1868 when the son of a white judge tried to shoot him down on the streets of Jackson. Caldwell fired back and killed his attacker. He was tried by an all-white jury and acquitted on the ground of self-defense. He was the first black to kill a white in Mississippi and go free.

Caldwell became one of the two blacks on the Hinds County Board of Police. It was an important office for, in addition to police duties, the Board also levied the county taxes. Caldwell served until elected to the senate of the first Reconstruction legislature in 1870. Now in the center of state politics, his support was heavily relied on by Senator and then Governor Ames.

The other two leaders were among the eight black preachers who sat in the convention. J. Aaron Moore had organized Methodist churches in the east-central portion of the state. With Meridian his base, he later became an influential state senator. When he left politics, he opened a blacksmith shop in Jackson.

Henry P. Jacobs, a Baptist preacher, organized Adams County for the Republicans. An Alabama slave, he learned his ABC's from a lunatic for whom he was caretaker. When he was able to read and write, Jacob forged a pass and escaped north with his family in 1856. He moved from Canada to Michigan and then, during the war, to Natchez. After serving in the convention, he was elected to the legislature.

The central black leader in the convention was Rev. T. W. Stringer. He came to Vicksburg late in 1865 to supervise the missions of the African Methodist Church. Earlier he had shown great skill and energy in organizing religious and fraternal groups in Ohio and Canada. "Wherever he went in the state," said one historian, "churches, lodges, benevolent societies, and political machines sprang up and flourished." In 1867, he introduced the Masonic order to the blacks of Mississippi, organizing lodges in several places. In 1870, Stringer was elected to the state senate, where he played a very active role.

A plantation slave became another of Missis-

Hiram R. Revels of Mississippi is sworn in as U.S. Senator in 1870, the first black elected to that office.

sippi's outstanding leaders. Born near Holly Springs
in 1846, James Hill was given his first schooling by
two daughters of the plantation owner. He kept
studying while working in a railroad shop. He
never was able to go to a formal school, but he
helped send his younger brother Frank to Oberlin
College.

Hired as sergeant-at-arms for the House in the
first Reconstruction legislature, Hill was elected as
a member the next year. He was not an orator. His
path up was made by his efficient and intelligent
political skills. He was elected to secretary of state,
an office he filled for three years. He then became
Vicksburg's postmaster and later was collector of
internal revenue. After leaving politics he made a
new and successful career in business.

Two Mississippi blacks won great prominence
nationally when they were elected to the United
States Senate. Neither was native-born. Hiram
Rhoads Revels, born free in North Carolina in 1827,
was educated there at a school run by a black
woman. He worked as a barber, until, to advance his
education, he went to seminaries in Indiana and
Ohio. He took his degree at Knox College in Illinois
and was ordained an African Methodist Episcopal
preacher in 1845. Revels taught school, lectured,
and preached in the Midwest. Then he became

principal of a school for blacks in Maryland. During
the Civil War, he helped recruit black troops in
Maryland and Missouri. He joined the Union Army
as chaplain of a black regiment in Mississippi. After
the war, he settled in Natchez as presiding elder
of the Methodist Episcopal Church. He served on
the city council until asked by John R. Lynch to
run for the state senate. When elected, he opened
the legislature's session with a prayer delivered
with a style and force that made a great impression
on all his hearers.

One of the legislature's first duties was to fill
the vacant seat left in the U.S. Senate when Jefferson Davis quit to become President of the Confederacy. Only one year was left of the unexpired
term. The Republicans agreed the seat should go to
a black. Revels was the choice of his black fellow
legislators.

When he arrived in Washington, some senators, appalled at the notion of a black man sitting
with them—and in Jefferson Davis' seat, at that—
tried to delay his acceptance. But after three days
of debate, a speech by Senator Charles Sumner in
his behalf ended the argument, and Revels was admitted as the first black man to serve in the Senate.
His dignity, his talent as a speaker, his devotion to
work, and his voting record earned him high regard
during his year in office.

Born a slave, Blanche K. Bruce was elected to the U.S. Senate at 33, the first black to serve a full term.

When he left the Senate, he was appointed
president of Alcorn College, Mississippi's new state
college for blacks. But under pressure, he proved
to be a timid man. In the crucial and bloody state
election of 1875, he campaigned for the Democrats.
After the election, he wrote President Grant to
say the Democratic victory was fairly won and the
best thing for his people. The grateful Democrats
promptly reappointed him president of Alcorn
College. Revels died in 1901.

The other senator from Mississippi, Blanche
Kelso Bruce, was the first black ever to serve a full
term in that office (and the only one until the election of Edward Brooke of Massachusetts in 1966).
He was born a slave in 1841, on a plantation in
Prince Edward County, Virginia. As the companion
of his master's son William, Blanche was allowed to
share in the lessons given by William's tutor.

The planter moved with his slaves to Missouri,
where Bruce learned the printing trade. When the
rebels fired on Fort Sumter, Bruce decided it was
time to emancipate himself. He got away to Kansas
and freedom. He taught in the state's first grade
school for blacks while he took advanced lessons
from a private tutor. He studied at Oberlin College,
but had to leave in a year when his money ran out.
For two years he wandered through the Midwest

At 22, the ex-slave John Roy Lynch was elected to the state legislature. A year later Mississippi sent him to Congress, where he served three terms.

and into the South, finally reaching Mississippi early in 1869.

A tall, powerfully built man, with ambition and the abilities to fulfill it, he began on a political career. The freedmen needed leaders, and Bruce found himself in the right place at the right time. He earned experience as election commissioner and as sergeant-at-arms in the state senate. In 1871, he was elected sheriff and tax assessor of Bolivar County, where he settled. A little later he became county superintendent of schools. He bought a 640-acre plantation and within a few years was rated a prosperous planter. He began a campaign for the Senate, and with solid support from the state's black leaders, was elected. In March 1875, he took his seat in Washington. He was now thirty-four years old. With the backing of powerful Radical Republicans, he was given good committee posts and soon became active on the floor.

In the first two speeches he made, Senator Bruce fought to protect the freedmen's rights. Reconstruction was already nearing its end and attacks on black voters and candidates were reaching a bloody climax. Bruce protested the proposal to remove federal troops from the South. He was concerned for the rights of all minorities, as well as his own people. He tried to prod the federal government toward a more progressive policy for the In-

Senator Revels (seated on the left) and the six other blacks who were the first to serve in Congress during Reconstruction.

dians, and he opposed the attempt to keep Chinese from entering the country. He worked for flood control on the Mississippi River, for aid to education, and for railroad construction.

His six years in the Senate ended when he was forty. He left his seat with so good a reputation that many influential people, including some Southerners, recommended him for a place in President Garfield's cabinet. Instead, Garfield made him Register of the U.S. Treasury, the highest post to which a black had yet been appointed. Later Bruce served as recorder of deeds for the District of Columbia and then once again as Register of the Treasury. He died in office in 1898.

10

Trouble ahead

It was in the towns and counties that Mississippians
met political power face to face. The state capital
in Jackson or the national capital in Washington
were far off. What a man's elected representatives
did in those distant places might be important, but
he didn't see it happening. Here at home, however,
he went by the sheriff's office almost daily; he sat
in the county courthouse to watch trials; he pushed
through the tax assessor's door to complain about
the rates.

So it was in these places that Mississippi saw black power operate during Reconstruction. The sheriff, in those days, was the most important county official. Under the Reconstruction constitution he had many political powers. It was the sheriff who selected trial juries, appointed election registrars, collected the state and county taxes.

His pay came in the form of fees for his services. In some counties, the fees ran as high as $20,000 a year. The average was about $5000.

Where the freedmen were in the majority, the sheriff was often a black man. De Soto, Issaquena, Jefferson, Hinds, Bolivar, Coahoma, Claiborne, Warren, and Washington were among the dozen or so Mississippi counties which had black sheriffs at one time or another during Reconstruction. Some served as long as four terms. More frequently, however, the post was held by a Northern white.

Some of the counties had black treasurers, and several had black superintendents of education. Blanche K. Bruce held both these jobs in Bolivar County. Occasionally there were blacks working as county clerks, too.

Very important in local government were the boards of supervisors and the justices of the peace. The supervisors had to oversee the work of erecting or repairing public buildings and bridges; the need for them was great after the wreckage of war. The board also assessed taxes and decided how to spend them, supervised roads and highways, awarded contracts, negotiated loans, appointed levee commissioners. The justices heard and decided on the great number of lesser offenses which occurred in their county. They held sway over civil suits up to $150, and all petty crimes such as larceny, trespass, assault and battery. With freedmen now allowed to bring suit, testify, and serve on juries, the courts at least doubled their business.

In some counties, such as Issaquena and Madison, at times every member of the board of supervisors was black. Charges of extravagance and corruption were constantly made against the blacks. Yazoo, a large and wealthy county in the Mississippi Valley region, was a special target. Its population was black by a large majority. The sheriff's post was held by the white man from Wisconsin, Colonel Morgan, who had married black Carrie Highgate.

The clerks and treasurer of Yazoo were black, and so were three of the five supervisors. Charges were made that Morgan and the blacks had plunged the county deeply into debt. But on the contrary, the record showed that Morgan's "radicals," by 1875, had finished all the repairs on the county highways and bridges and built new bridges. They had

Freedmen cast their ballots. In many counties of Mississippi they elected black sheriffs, supervisors, justices, treasurers, and school superintendents.

improved the poor-farm buildings and put the farm itself back into cultivation so that it was nearly self-supporting. The size and security of the jail had been enlarged, a new courthouse had been built and paid for, new sidewalks, pavements, and gutters had been made in Yazoo City, and a new

fire engine provided. Sixty new schools had been
built and paid for. And the tax levy, in that whole
period, had never gone above 2.5 percent, a very
slight increase. The Morgans did well for the
county, but they lost their own fortune.

What upset the old planters especially was the
fact that those who enjoyed the honor and power
of local office, as well as those who voted them into
office, were so often "poor nobodies." Most of the
black officials had never owned property before.
How could they, as slaves? And now too, only a
small part of them had real estate. It enraged the
local whites to see the common people, especially
blacks, administering the affairs of government.

Black policemen, too, upset the whites. If a
man's job was to enforce the law, he represented
power in a very direct way. Whites could hardly
believe their eyes when they first saw black men
in uniform policing their communities. "Negroes
ought not to be put in a position to discharge con-
stabulary functions which it is proper for white
men to exercise," complained Ethelbert Barksdale,
one of the old leaders of the state. The white race,
he said, was "not in the habit of being dominated by
the colored race."

Blacks served on juries, too. It had begun in
1868 when General Ames ruled that race or color

could no longer be a bar to serving on a jury. His order was made law by the Reconstruction legislature of 1870. Native whites were horrified. One of them, Franklin Montgomery, described his reaction the first time he found himself on a jury with blacks: "I was on the panel for the week, and so great was my disgust that I at once applied for, and easily obtained, a license to practice law, thus escaping what I thought would have been a degradation."

That feeling lasted for a while, but gradually whites began serving willingly with blacks, and, as Wharton noted, "found them generally kind hearted, just, and honest." Counties that were half black and half white in population divided their juries accordingly, and where blacks were in the majority, they usually held a majority on the juries, too.

It was amazing to see how, out of nowhere, the black men had come to lead their people. From despised slaves they were transformed almost overnight into makers and doers.

Most of the new leaders were not men who had any responsibility in the slavery period. A man like B. T. Montgomery, managing the big Davis plantations, was very uncommon. The majority of native blacks who won office had been slaves working in the towns—blacksmiths, carpenters, clerks, waiters, servants—and preachers, too, of course.

They got their schooling in politics by working in the Loyal Leagues. These had sprung up in almost every black belt community during the war. With a start from the whites and blacks who had come from the North, they quickly became both political and social centers. Usually they held meetings twice a month. Besides discussing political, school, and church affairs, they danced and played games. They met in churches or schools. High points of their activity were the political banquets and barbecues. During elections they organized political parades. Decorated with sashes and badges, they marched proudly through the streets to the beat of their drum corps. With colorful floats, flaring torches, and illuminated pictures, they carried their programs to the people.

When election time came around, the leagues rounded up their followers and brought them in large groups to the polls. In many places the black Republican voters would flood into the polls in the morning, leaving the afternoons to the white Democrats.

By 1873, the Republicans in Mississippi were at the peak of their power. They had swept the election of 1872 and had put Republicans in five of the six congressional seats. Now the black people,

Campaigning for political office. The majority of blacks elected to office in Mississippi were ex-slaves.

whose great numbers made the party strong, felt it was time they had a larger share of political power. Since it was their votes which put Republicans into office, why shouldn't more of their people be nominated? At least in proportion to their number? A black newspaper, the Vicksburg *Plain Dealer*, pointed out that it was tired of the old game, where white men always held the offices, while black men did the voting.

This demand, loudly voiced, led to a split among the Republicans. Thousands of whites in the party, and most of the white leaders who came from the old wealthy and educated class, refused to accept the growing black power. They were alarmed by the prospect of more and more black officeholders. Under Alcorn's guidance, they formed another party, and were joined by some of the Democrats.

In the next election, Alcorn, who was in the U.S. Senate, ran again for governor, opposing Adelbert Ames, who headed the Republican ticket favored by the blacks. The Ames slate won easily, putting three blacks into the top seven state offices. The lieutenant governor, the secretary of state, and the superintendent of education, were all blacks. A fourth black was chosen speaker of the house. Fifty-five of the 115 members of the lower house were black, and nine of the thirty-seven state senators.

It was a big increase in the number of blacks in state government. The record showed they did just as well as any of the earlier, and whiter, legislatures. Traveling in the South in 1874, Edward

King wrote that the black officeholders he met in Mississippi made a powerful impression on him as "worthy, intelligent, and likely to progress." He saw many "exceedingly capable" blacks in government, he reported in his book, *The Great South.*

It would be ridiculous to claim that Mississippi's Reconstruction governments were perfect. There was some waste and some corruption in this state, as well as in all the reconstructed states. The South was a victim of the same immorality in public affairs that the North suffered from in the postwar years. There was graft and thievery in New York and Washington and in almost every state legislature in America. Dishonest profits were easy at a time when business was booming, and the government was pouring money into its expansion. Men got rich overnight from railroad deals. Votes were sometimes bought to get franchises or land grants that would enrich corporations.

The South, during Reconstruction, was the focus of national attention. Most of the graft was on a small scale, but it was blown up big. The Democrats and their newspapers loved to blame public immorality on what they called the "nigger" governments. They pinned the label of "The Dreadful Decade" on Reconstruction.

But the two Southern historians who made the

closest study of Mississippi said the label is false. "The Republican state regime left a remarkable record of honesty," wrote Wharton. The other scholar, James W. Garner, wrote: "So far as the conduct of the state officials who were entrusted with the custody of public funds is concerned, it may be said that there were no great embezzlements or other cases of misappropriation during the period of Republican rule."

Wharton added that the blacks, with their white colleagues, "gave to the state a government of greatly expanded functions at a cost that was low in comparison with that of almost any other state."

But promising as black Reconstruction's record was, there were grave signs of trouble ahead.

11

A dream destroyed

The big trouble began in 1874, but it had started much earlier.

From the beginning of Reconstruction in Mississippi, there were many whites who accepted the results of the war. They wanted their state back in the Union and hoped for peace and prosperity. They were willing for the freedmen to have the rights the amended Constitution had granted them. They were willing to join blacks in the Republican Party as long as the blacks accepted white leadership.

But they would not deal with the blacks as political equals. It made no difference how capable and honest the blacks were.

By 1873, it was plain that the freedmen were determined to assert their leadership in the Republican Party. Most of the whites dropped out. The freedmen were alone. Massed against them now were the planters, the white middle class, the poor whites, and the small white farmers. All the whites had been raised to believe the black was an inferior creature who had to be kept down. The whites must be supreme. The race line had always been there, but by 1873 it was being drawn into a noose that would strangle Reconstruction.

The old cry for white supremacy was raised. The whites no longer feared the federal government. Popular support for the Radical program had faded. Northerners lost interest in Reconstruction as they turned to other problems. A terrible depression seized the country in 1873. It grew deeper and deeper until there were millions of unemployed. With hard times, the Republicans began to lose ground.

The victims of the depression blamed the party in power. In the state and congressional elections of 1874, the Democrats gained great victories. They won control of the House of Representatives and left the Republicans with only a small majority in the Senate. And Democrats took control of most state governments, North and South.

It was a crushing blow for the Republican Party in the South. Many of the native whites who had supported it began deserting it for the party of the winners.

Now only four Southern states were still governed by Republicans. They were Florida, Louisiana, South Carolina, and Mississippi. The Democrats had restored white supremacy everywhere else.

This was the time to strike, said the Democrats in Mississippi. They no longer needed to be cautious for they were sure the national government would not interfere.

Attacks on the black people became more bitter and violent in the press. The Yazoo City *Banner* announced, "Mississippi is a white man's country, and by the Eternal God we'll rule it." The Handsboro *Democrat* demanded "a white man's government by white men, for the benefit of white men."

They called themselves "White Liners." They believed, as one observer said, that any white man, no matter how bad, was better than any black man,

The Democrats tried every possible means, including fraud and force, to overthrow the Radical Republicans. Here, White Leaguers use guns to keep blacks from the polls.

no matter how good. Their aim was to smash black power. They wanted to break Republican control of state government at any cost.

They tried economic pressure first. No blacks who voted Republican could hope for work, they said. To show they meant business, Vicksburg merchants fired black porters and hired whites. The Vicksburg & Meridian Railroad did the same with black mail clerks. The newspapers urged their readers to buy only from white Democrats.

At the same time, they tried to bribe blacks into joining the Democratic Party. They promised protection and jobs. They offered picnics and parades, bands and barbecues, but very few Uncle Toms came around.

Threats of violence were tried next. Terror, of course, was not a new weapon. (Teachers, black and white, had been among its victims all along.) At Meridian, in 1871, about thirty blacks were killed and the local Republican government overthrown. It was this mass violence which led President Grant to inform Congress that neither life nor property was secure in the South, and especially in Mississippi. Congress had responded with an anti-Klan law that slowed down the terror.

But now, in 1874, Democrats throughout the state felt it safe to defy federal laws protecting civil

rights. They organized private military companies
to overthrow the Radical regimes. The rifle companies were really the armed wing of the Democratic Party. They were controlled by James Z.
George, a Confederate general who was the party's
campaign manager. Later he became chief justice
of the state supreme court and U.S. Senator. Although their goal was political, they were trained
to use force. Their blueprint for political violence
came to be known as the "Shotgun Plan." Almost
half the whites of voting age were enrolled in the
movement. One outfit, for instance, had cavalry,
infantry, cannon, rifles, shotguns, and pistols. They
would sweep into a town, stop all blacks and publicly write down their names in "Dead Books."
They paraded coffins through the streets, with the
names of Radical leaders painted on them, and such
labels as "Dead, damned, and delivered." They had
passed the old secret Ku Klux stage. Now they were
an armed force out in the open, wanting the blacks
to know Mississippi's whites meant to destroy Republican rule.

Often they carried out violence with the help
of companies from the nearby states of Alabama,
Arkansas, and Georgia.

In Vicksburg in 1874, seven of the military units,
helped by 160 armed whites from Louisiana, took

control of the election. Blacks were kept away from the polls, and the Republicans were of course defeated. Firing broke out and at least thirty-five blacks were killed. Two whites died. From as far away as Trinity, Texas, came a telegram to the White Liners: "Do you want any men? Can raise good crowd within four hours to kill out your negroes."

Said the Vicksburg *Monitor: The same tactics that saved Vicksburg will surely save the State, and no other will.* The newspaper was pointing the way to victory in the state election set for November, 1875. The Mississippians would vote for members of Congress, the state legislature, and county officers.

Month after month the terror went on. Again in Vicksburg, two blacks killed; no whites. In Louisville, two blacks wounded; no whites hurt. In Macon, thirteen blacks killed; no whites.

In September, 1875, the rifle companies took over Yazoo County. By plan, they lynched every black leader in each supervisor's district.

Three days later, the Republicans held a political picnic at Clinton in Hinds County. It was a Baptist seminary town and the home of Charles Caldwell, the slave blacksmith who had risen to state senator. He was county chairman of the Re-

publican Party and a candidate for reelection to the
senate. He invited a Democrat to debate the issues
at the picnic.

While the Republican was speaking, a white
man named Thompson drew a pistol, and pointing
it at one of the blacks, began cursing him. Caldwell
slipped up to the white and said, "For God's sake,
don't disturb the meeting." Thompson would not
listen. Then other whites drew their guns and
shooting began. Thompson poured several shots into the crowd and the firing became general. Observers estimated that from twenty to thirty blacks
were killed, and many wounded. Two whites were
killed and four wounded.

The whites were in a bloodthirsty rage.
Alarmed at the terror unleashed, the blacks hid in
the woods and swamps, or fled ten miles off to
Jackson, seeking the protection of Governor Ames.
The local whites telegraphed to Vicksburg for more
men, and that night a special train brought in a
white rifle company called the Modocs. For four
days they hunted down black and white Republican leaders, killing from thirty to fifty of them.

A band of Modocs raided Caldwell's home as
soon as they reached Clinton. Caldwell was in
Jackson, but his wife was in the house, nursing two
wounded blacks. The gang stayed all night, stole

all they could carry, and when they left at dawn, their captain, Tinney, told Mrs. Caldwell they meant to kill her husband if it took one year or six. "We have orders to kill him," Tinney said, "and we are going to do it because he belongs to the Republican Party and sticks up for these Negroes. We are going to have the South back in our own charge."

When they left the senator's home (as Mrs. Caldwell told a congressional investigating committee later) "they went to a house where there was an old man, a feeble old man, named Bob Beasley, and they shot him all to pieces. And then they went to Mr. Willis' and took out a man, named Gamaliel Brown, and shot him all to pieces . . . and they goes out to Sam Jackson's, president of the [Republican] club, and they shot him all to pieces . . . and they went out to Alfred Hastings . . . and they shot Alfred Hastings all to pieces, another man named Ben Jackson, and they go out and shoot one or two further up on the Madison road . . . Lewis Russell and Moses Hill. They were around that morning killing people before breakfast . . . They didn't intend to leave anyone alive they could catch."

One of the whites they went after that morning was William P. Haffa, a quiet but courageous Philadelphian who had come to Mississippi in 1870 with his family. He had been raising cotton and corn in Hinds County for only a few months when he was threatened by the whites for showing friendship to the freedmen. He would make friends with whom he liked, he said. His white neighbors' anger swelled when Haffa was elected justice of the peace with black support. One day the whites kidnapped Haffa from his home, tied him to a tree, and lashed him for almost two hours. They knocked his wife so violently against a wall she never got over the injuries. Senator Caldwell took her to Jackson and paid fifty dollars for her medical treatment.

Every few months now, the Haffas were insulted or attacked, and once even their little boy was shot at. One man called Haffa out of his house at night and when he appeared cocked a pistol at him. Haffa snatched it out of the man's hand, forced him down from his horse, and locked him in the cotton house till the morning.

Saying they were afraid they were going to lose him, Haffa's black neighbors provided him with guards who stuck by him even when he went from his house to his stable.

When the Reconstruction school program opened, Mrs. Haffa taught classes for blacks, working with the children in the day and the adults at night. She became secretary of their political club

which met in the schoolhouse near her home. Later
the freedmen asked Mr. Haffa if he too would teach
school, and he agreed. Early that bloody September
of 1875, his black neighbors came to Haffa and told
him the whites were saying loudly they would destroy him. "Don't you feel afraid of your life?" they
asked him. "No," he said, "I'm not timid. I don't
suppose they will harm me now, after we have been
living here so many years, and they have attempted
it so often."

Early on the same Monday morning the
Modocs raided the Haffas' home. The Haffas were
awakened by the furious barking of their dog.

"Who's there?" Haffa cried out.

"We'll let you know who's there!" a voice yelled
back.

Haffa looked out the window and saw about
seventy-five men surrounding the house, all heavily
armed. They tried to force the lock and when that
failed, tore up a fence rail and battered the door
down. Mosely, the Singer Sewing Machine agent
for the district, rushed in and choked off Mrs.
Haffa's screams. Through the window came two
shots that hit Haffa, fired by Sid Whitehead, the
man who owned the land they rented. The whites
fled, and Mrs. Haffa and her daughter carried the
wounded man to his bed, while her son rushed

out to get help from their black neighbors. As
Haffa lay dying, Whitehead came in and refused to
let anyone send for a doctor. "It's no use," he said,
"he'll die anyhow." Almost gone, Haffa looked at
his murderer and said, "Let me have water . . .
that's all I'll ask for." Then he laid his head on his
wife's shoulder, and died.

Every Republican leader they found, they
killed that morning. It went on for three more days,
the blacks begging the authorities for arms to defend themselves, but in vain. All the while, a small
unit of federal troops stood by in Clinton, doing
nothing to stop the wholesale slaughter. When it
was over, the Army officers and the local gentry sat
down to a pleasant dinner together.

Governor Ames issued a proclamation calling
on all the extra-legal armed companies to disband.
They laughed at him. The next day Ames wired
President Grant for help. But Grant, through his
attorney general, wired back to Ames that "the
whole public are tired of the annual autumnal out-
breaks in the South."

It was the signal that the federal government
had given up on Reconstruction.

Ames' last hope was to organize his own state
militia to protect the citizens' voting rights. Seven
companies were formed, five black and two white.

Charles Caldwell was the first to organize one, and became its captain. Governor Ames asked him to deliver arms from the Jackson arsenal to new militiamen recruited at Edwards' Depot, about thirty miles west of the capital. On October 9, at the head of 102 black militia, Caldwell marched along the public highway to deliver the weapons. His men bivouacked overnight near Clinton, the scene of the recent killings. Adding the new company to his force, plus another hundred who fell in at Brownsville, Caldwell marched back to Jackson with flags flying, drums beating, and bayonets ready.

It was an incredibly courageous act of leadership, to parade thus through blood-crazed enemy territory. They could expect to be ambushed at every turn in the road. But nothing happened. The Democratic leaders had rushed word to every village that Caldwell didn't scare. If attacked, he would fight to the death. And open warfare could mean federal intervention and disaster for the white supremacy cause.

Caldwell had demonstrated armed black support for the governor. But Ames, believing the cause was doomed, and losing all heart, ordered the companies to disband and give up their arms. He feared if he used them it would bring on a race war in which the blacks would be slaughtered.

Three days later Ames signed a "Peace Agree-
ment" with the Democrats' leaders. Ames agreed
to disband the state militia while the other side
pledged not to use violence or fraud in the coming
elections.

How lightly the Democrats took their pledge
could be seen in their newspapers. They bore the
slogan: "Carry the election peaceably if we can,
forcibly if we must."

Caldwell told the governor the peace treaty
was a joke. It left the Republicans defenseless in
the face of an armed and pitiless enemy. And the
Democrats were not stopping their program of
fraud and violence for one moment.

The day before the election the Democrats
hung six blacks in Yazoo City.

On election day, the Democrats did whatever
they liked to guarantee their victory. In some
places, the only blacks they let vote were those who
showed Democratic ballots, or who came to the
polls with white Democrats. Many blacks who
carried Republican ballots were shot at or beaten
back from the polls.

In Monroe County, the Democrats tore down
a bridge and posted pickets to keep the freedmen
from reaching the polls. But when they came by

other routes, the Democrats surrounded them with cavalry and infantry, trained cannon on them, "and then sent a strong arm squad into the crowd to beat the negroes over the head," the Aberdeen *Examiner* reported.

Charles Caldwell, begged by a friend to stay away from the polls for fear he would be murdered, refused. He voted.

And so did tens of thousands of other brave blacks.

In fact, close study of the election returns by the historian David Donald shows *more* blacks voted than ever before. The freedmen were *not* frightened out of voting. If they had been, said Donald, there should have been fewer Republican ballots cast than in former years. But that was not the case. The Republican vote of 67,000 was almost as big as in previous elections.

What, then, accounts for the Democratic victory? The fact that thousands of scalawags—native whites, mostly followers of Alcorn—who used to vote Republican, had deserted the party to vote on the color line. The Southern whites were now united in one party strong enough to win.

There was cheating too, of course. In Yazoo City, for example, where 2427 Republican votes were counted in 1873, this time seven were counted.

In five delta counties, the Democratic vote was so great it was plain the planters had simply "voted" their black tenants for the Democratic Party.

Still, the Shotgun Plan had not intimidated the blacks. They managed, in spite of everything, to reelect John R. Lynch to Congress, and send twenty-one blacks to the state legislature.

Men like Charles Caldwell were not forgiven or forgotten for their courage and independence.

On Christmas Day, 1875, Caldwell had his dinner at home and then walked into town about sundown. A man named Buck Cabell came up to him and asked to have a drink with him. Caldwell said he didn't feel much like it, but Cabell insisted on it as a Christmas treat. So the two men went down into the cellar of Chilton's store. The drinks were poured, and the men raised their glasses and clinked them together. At the ring of the glasses, a shot blasted through the cellar window and struck Caldwell in the back of the head. Plainly the tap of the glasses was the signal for the ambush to be triggered. Caldwell fell to the ground, calling for help. Men with guns stood beyond the window in the street above, but no one answered his appeal. Finally Mr. Nelson, a preacher, came to the cellar door hesitantly and called down that he would help if Caldwell would promise not to shoot him. "I won't hurt you," Caldwell said. "Just take me out of the cellar. I want to die in the open air, not like a dog closed up."

Nelson carried him up to the street. Caldwell was close to death from the single shot. He asked the preacher to take him home so that he could see his wife before he died. The Caldwell house was nearby, but the men refused to let him be moved. "We'll save him while we've got him," they yelled. "Dead men tell no tales."

Caldwell would not beg. He pulled his coat together as he lay there and said, "Remember, when you kill me you kill a gentleman and a brave man. Never say you killed a coward. I want you to remember it when I am gone."

At that the men standing over him began pumping bullet after bullet into him. Thirty or forty times the guns roared, the force of the bullets whipping the body over and over in the dirt. Just then Caldwell's brother Sam, a peaceable man known never to use a gun, came riding in from the country. They shot him down off his horse and killed him, too.

The moon had just risen, and at home Mrs. Caldwell sitting by her window heard her church bell ring. The moment the bell tolled she knew what it meant. So did the whole black community.

At the signal of danger, the young men poured through doors and leaped from windows, rushing to the church where 150 guns were stored. All that night they stood guard over their homes.

The bodies of the Caldwell brothers were brought to the house and laid out on a bed. At one o'clock in the morning a train came in from Vicksburg with the Modocs, who marched straight to the Caldwell home. "They went into where the two dead bodies laid," said Mrs. Caldwell, "and they cursed them, those dead bodies there, and they danced and threw open the melodeon and sang all their songs, and challenged my husband to get up and fight."

It was the only time Charles Caldwell did not fight back.

12

The price
we pay

The shotgun policy had worked. The new Mississippi legislature met in January, 1876, with the Democrats solidly back in power. They removed the lieutenant governor from office and forced the resignation of the superintendent of education and Governor Ames. Ames had lost all desire to fight and left the state.

Said President Grant, "Mississippi is governed today by officials chosen through fraud and violence such as would scarcely be credited to savages, much less to a civilized and Christian people." It was a good statement to get on the record, but the President had done nothing to stop it from happening.

Many blacks, despairing of any future in Mississippi, wanted to move to the West or emigrate to Africa. Thousands managed to leave, but the great mass stayed.

They did not drop out of politics, although they knew what happened in 1875 would happen again. And so it did, in the 1876 election. The Democrats used violence and fraud again and swept to victory. They won all the seats in Congress and control of every county but four. The 1876 presidential election marked the end of Reconstruction.

The North, made an industrial giant by the war, had new values and goals. It was no longer interested in anything that might disturb its growth. It was ready to make peace with the South at any price. The black people knew that price was the loss of their political and civil rights.

The two candidates for the presidency were unimpressive politicians. The Democratic Party put up Samuel J. Tilden, governor of New York, and the Republicans nominated Rutherford B. Hayes, governor of Ohio.

In several places—Florida, Louisiana, and South

Carolina, particularly—the Democrats borrowed the Mississippi Shotgun Plan as a model for "redeeming" their states for white supremacy. Their party clubs were converted into rifle companies. The South Carolina leader, General M. W. Gary, advised that "Every Democrat must feel honor bound to control the vote of at least one Negro, by intimidation, purchase, keeping him away or as each individual may determine, how he may best accomplish it."

In Florida, said a black leader, the Democrats made it clear that "all colored people that voted the Republican ticket were to be starved out the next year."

With force or fraud controlling many polling places that November, the election returns were bound to be challenged. Early results indicated that Tilden seemed to have barely defeated Hayes, and the white Southerners were jubilant. But a dispute broke out over the returns from Florida, Louisiana, and South Carolina, where Mississippi methods had been copied to overcome the typical Republican majorities. The election boards of these states, with black men sitting on them, threw out ballots spoiled by terror and fraud. When the electoral votes of these three states were given to Hayes, it meant his victory.

The white South refused to accept it. Congressman Henry Watterson of Kentucky threatened an armed march of a hundred thousand men on Washington to see that Tilden was inaugurated. Talk of another civil war crackled in the press. To prevent two presidents from claiming they were legally elected, Congress established an electoral commission made up of fifteen men, five each from the House, the Senate, and the Supreme Court. They voted strictly by party on every point of the dispute, and decided by eight to seven in favor of Hayes.

Tilden's supporters bitterly opposed the outcome, and staged a filibuster in the House of Representatives to prevent the official count of the electoral votes according to the commission's decision. It looked like the country would reach inauguration day with no president at all or with two men claiming the White House.

The nation was in great turmoil. Business leaders, fearful of the effects of the explosive situation upon trade and commerce, feverishly worked for "peace at any price."

Influential Republicans and Democrats held a series of secret meetings through the winter months, to work out a bargain. The white South's attitude was put bluntly by L. Q. C. Lamar, a wealthy political leader from Mississippi, now in Congress. He said it was more important that the South should have local self-government than that the President should be a Democrat. In other words, what Southern Democrats wanted was to be let alone. If the federal administration would keep its hands off the South, allowing whites to manage their affairs (meaning the blacks) their own way, then a Republican could enjoy the White House.

And what the Mississippian wanted became the heart of the bargain that brought about acceptance of the commission's decision.

The Republicans agreed to remove the last of the federal troops from the South. The South was promised "home rule" and the federal economic help it badly needed.

In return, the Southern Democrats agreed to accept the Republican Hayes as President. And they promised to treat the blacks fairly.

Hayes moved into the White House in March, 1877. The federal troops marched out of the South. The white Democrats were now in complete control.

Reconstruction was over.

It had not lasted very long in any state. In Georgia and North Carolina, only two years, in Mississippi, six years. In South Carolina—the longest—seven years.

Frederick Douglass told why it failed. In 1880, in a speech to black people in Elmira, New York, he said:

Our reconstruction measures were radically defective. They left the former slave completely in the power of the old master, the loyal citizen in the hands of the disloyal rebel against the government. . . .
To the freedmen was given the machinery of liberty, but there was denied them the steam to put it in motion. They were given the uniform of soldiers, but no arms; they were called citizens, but left subjects; they were called free, but left almost slaves.

The central failure, Douglass said, was the refusal of Congress to give the freedmen a chance to obtain good land of their own. "Could the nation have been induced to listen to those stalwart Republicans, Thaddeus Stevens and Charles Sumner, some of the evils which we now suffer would have been averted. The Negro would not today be on his knees, as he is, supplicating the old master class to give him leave to toil. . . . He would not now be swindled out of his hard earnings by money orders for wages with no money in them. Nor would he now be leaving the South as from a doomed city, seeking a home in the uncongenial North, but tilling his native soil in comparative independence."

Were the years of Reconstruction a total loss?

The great mass of freedmen did see an improvement in their living conditions. They had better homes and furnishings, food, and clothing. They had built their own schools and churches, and paid for their teachers and ministers. They had started their own fire companies, reading clubs, burial and insurance associations, military companies, and fraternal groups.

Their gains were of course not as much as the whites. But measured by where they had stood in slavery, Reconstruction was in this sense a success. The black man's many political achievements, temporary though they were, made possible his economic advance.

As for freedom, in that brief span of Reconstruction, blacks learned how to use it. From slaves they made themselves into farmers and businessmen, students and teachers, lawyers and bishops, jurors and judges, sheriffs and senators.

They organized, they learned, they grew, they fought. It was not their fault that they lost. It was a failure of the whole American people. Nor were blacks the only ones who lost. The *nation* suffered a terrible defeat when Reconstruction was abandoned. It set back the cause of freedom and democracy for generations. We still pay the price for it.

Today there are many thousands of new Reconstructionists.

They are part of a civil rights movement that began in the early 1950s when a series of historic Supreme Court decisions affirmed the basic rights of democracy for all. But from the school desegregation ruling of 1954 down to today it has been clear that noble words on paper are not enough. Legal victories on the racial front have been ignored or defied. In this new Reconstruction, the freedom fighters have used ballots, boycotts, picket lines, sit ins, marches, demonstrations, and ghetto uprisings to win gains that should always have been the right of free citizens of these United States.

Black youths, especially, are impatient with the slow pace of change. In the North as well as the South, they demand full membership in American democracy. City, state, and federal governments offer token programs to reduce the tensions—in housing, recreation, education, jobs and job training —but little of substance has been done to get at the underlying causes of the fury in the streets.

Only when black Americans have full and equal participation in the possibilities of this society will the Reconstruction that began over a hundred years ago be completed.

Bibliography

Note: Starred books are available in paperback editions.

* Allen, James S., *Reconstruction, The Battle for Democracy,* New York: International, 1937.

* Bennett, Lerone, *Black Power U.S.A.,* Baltimore: Penguin, 1969.

* Berger, Morroe, *Equality by Statute,* New York: Doubleday, 1967.

* Botkin, B. A., *Lay My Burden Down,* Chicago: University of Chicago, 1945.

* Buckmaster, Henrietta, *Freedom Bound,* New York: Macmillan, 1965.

* Current, Richard N., *Reconstruction, 1865-1877,* Englewood Cliffs: Prentice-Hall, 1965.

* Dennett, John Richard, *The South As It Is: 1865-1866,* New York: Viking, 1967.

* DuBois, W. E. B., *Black Reconstruction,* New York: Harcourt, Brace, 1935.

* Fleming, Walter L., *Documentary History of Reconstruction,* New York: McGraw-Hill, 1966.

* Franklin, John Hope, *Reconstruction After the Civil War,* Chicago: University of Chicago, 1961.

Garner, James W., *Reconstruction in Mississippi,* Gloucester: Peter Smith, 1964.

Harris, William C., *Presidential Reconstruction in Mississippi,* Baton Rouge: Louisiana State University, 1967.

Hughes, Langston and Meltzer, Milton, *A Pictorial History of the Negro in America,* New York: Crown, 1968.

King, Edward, *The Great South,* Hartford: American, 1875.

Knox, Thomas W., *Camp-Fire and Cotton Field,* New York: Blelock, 1865.

Lynch, John R., *The Facts of Reconstruction,* New York: Arno, 1969.

* McKitrick, Eric L., *Andrew Johnson and Reconstruction,* Chicago: University of Chicago, 1960.

* McPherson, James M., *The Struggle for Equality,* Princeton: Princeton University, 1964.

* McWhiney, Grady, *Reconstruction and the Freedmen,* Chicago: Rand McNally, 1963.

* Meltzer, Milton, *In Their Own Words: A History of the American Negro, Vol. II, 1865-1916,* New York: Crowell, 1965.

Morgan, Albert T., *Yazoo,* New York: Russell and Russell, 1969.

* Reid, Whitelaw, *After the War, A Tour of the Southern States, 1865-1866*, New York: Harper, 1965.

* Rose, Willie Lee, *Rehearsal for Reconstruction, The Port Royal Experiment*, Indianapolis: Bobbs-Merrill, 1964.

* Shenton, James P., *The Reconstruction, A Documentary History, 1865-1877*, New York: Putnam, 1963.

* Singletary, Otis A., *Negro Militia and Reconstruction*, New York: McGraw-Hill, 1963.

Smith, Samuel D., *The Negro in Congress, 1870-1901*, Chapel Hill: University of North Carolina, 1943.

* Stampp, Kenneth M., *The Era of Reconstruction, 1865-1877*, New York: Knopf, 1965.

* Stampp, Kenneth M. and Litwack, Leon F., *Reconstruction: An Anthology of Revisionist Writings*, Baton Rouge: Louisiana State University, 1969.

Sydnor, Charles S., *Slavery in Mississippi*, New York: Appleton-Century, 1933.

Trowbridge, John T., *A Picture of the Desolated States and The Work of Restoration, 1866-1868*, Hartford: Stebbins, 1868.

Warren, Henry W., *Reminiscences of a Mississippi Carpetbagger*, Worcester: Davis, 1914.

Werstein, Irving, *This Wounded Land*, New York: Delacorte, 1968.

* Wharton, Vernon Lane, *The Negro in Mississippi, 1865-1890*, New York: Harper Torchbook, 1965.

* Wiley, Bell Irvin, *Southern Negroes, 1861-1865*, New Haven: Yale University, 1938.

* Williamson, Joel, *After Slavery: The Negro in South Caro-

lina During Reconstruction, 1861-1877, Chapel Hill: University of North Carolina, 1965.

* Woodward, C. Vann, *The Burden of Southern History*, New York: Vintage, 1961.
* Woodward, C. Vann, *Reunion and Reaction*, New York: Doubleday, 1956.

Biographies

* Douglass, Frederick, *Life and Times of Frederick Douglass*, New York: Collier, 1962.

Foner, Philip S., *Frederick Douglass*, New York: Citadel, 1964.

Meltzer, Milton, *Thaddeus Stevens and the Fight for Negro Rights*, New York: Crowell, 1967.

* Quarles, Benjamin, *Frederick Douglass*, Washington: Associated, 1948.
* Sterling, Dorothy, *Captain of the Planter, the Story of Robert Smalls*, New York: Doubleday, 1958.
* Sterling, Philip and Logan, Rayford, *Four Took Freedom* (includes short biographies of Frederick Douglass, Robert Smalls, and Blanche K. Bruce, major figures in Reconstruction), New York: Doubleday, 1967.

Novels

* Fast, Howard, *Freedom Road*, New York: Duell, Sloan, 1944.
* Walker, Margaret, *Jubilee*, Boston: Houghton Mifflin, 1966.

Modern Mississippi

* Belfrage, Sally, *Freedom Summer*, New York: Viking, 1965.

Lord, Walter, *The Past That Would Not Die*, New York: Harper & Row, 1965.

Meredith, James H., *Three Years in Mississippi*, Bloomington: Indiana University, 1966.

* Moody, Anne, *Coming of Age in Mississippi*, New York: Dial, 1968.

Silver, James W., *Mississippi: The Closed Society*, New York: Harcourt, 1964.

Smith, Frank E., *Congressman from Mississippi*, New York: Pantheon, 1964.

* Sutherland, Elizabeth, *Letters from Mississippi*, New York: McGraw-Hill, 1965.

Index